Wicked
DANVILLE

Wicked DANVILLE

LIQUOR AND LAWLESSNESS IN A SOUTHSIDE VIRGINIA CITY

FRANKIE Y. BAILEY AND ALICE P. GREEN

Charleston | London

THE
History
PRESS

Published by The History Press
Charleston, SC 29403
www.historypress.net

Cover images: A few of the young boys working in the cigarette factory, Danville (Virginia), 1911. *Courtesy of the Library of Congress*; the image of the men with the still is partially a Library of Congress image, parade of mill strikers. *Courtesy of the Clara Foundation and Schoolfield Preservation Society.*

Cover design and illustration by Karleigh Hambrick

First published 2011

Manufactured in the United States

ISBN 978.1.60949.037.9

Library of Congress Cataloging-in-Publication Data

Bailey, Frankie Y.
Wicked Danville : liquor and lawlessness in a Southside Virginia city / Frankie Y. Bailey and
Alice P. Green.
p. cm.
Includes bibliographical references.
ISBN 978-1-60949-037-9
1. Crime--Virginia--Danville--History--Anecdotes. 2. Scandals--Virginia--Danville--
History--Anecdotes. 3. Corruption--Virginia--Danville--History--Anecdotes. 4. Criminals-
-Virginia--Danville--Biography--Anecdotes. 5. Danville (Va.)--History--Anecdotes.
6. Danville (Va.)--Social conditions--Anecdotes. 7. Danville (Va.)--Moral conditions--
Anecdotes. 8. Danville (Va.)--Biography--Anecdotes. I. Green, Alice P., 1946- II. Title.
HV6795.D32B24 2011
364.109755'666--dc22
2011008305

Contents

CONTENTS

Acknowledgements

The authors would like to thank the people who graciously shared their time and resources when we were working on this book. Among them is Esther Goins, who introduced us to Clara Fountain, who then shared with us her knowledge and photographs of Danville. We want to thank Karen Oestreicher, president, and Rick Frederick, webmaster and archivist, of the Caswell County Historical Association, who provided us with information about several images and about details concerning the link between Caswell County tobacco farmers and Danville. We would like to thank Robert "Danny" Ricketts, local historian, for directing us to his website. Joyce Wilburn of the Danville Historical Society provided us with information and leads. The volunteer staff at the Danville Museum of Fine Arts and History took the time for a long visit with us when we stopped in. The reference staff at the Danville Public Library helped us to find the information we needed, as did the library staff at Danville Community College. The Danville Police Department provided us with images from the department website. We would also like to thank funeral director James Price, with whom we spent a fascinating hour.

We would like to offer our special thanks to the interlibrary loan staff at University at Albany (SUNY) and to the staff of the Library of Virginia, who were efficient, helpful and supportive as we searched for images of Danville and sought microfilm.

Frankie would like to thank her aunt, Catherine Holt, who opened her home to us.

Alice would like to thank her husband, Charles Touhey, who came along for the ride and did all of the driving.

Finally, we would like to thank our commissioning editor, Hannah Cassilly, and the fine staff of The History Press.

CHAPTER 1

Danville in Time and Place

THE DEATH OF REVEREND MOFFETT

In November 1892, Reverend John R. Moffett, a local minister and the editor of a prohibitionist newspaper, was shot by J.T. Clark, a former storekeeper, attorney and Democratic politician. Ambitious and dedicated, Moffett had been strong in his work for the prohibition cause. As he sought converts, he expanded his activities beyond his church in North Danville. In doing so, he made personal and political enemies.

In August 1889, Moffett had given a speech in nearby Chatham, the county seat of Pittsylvania County. To express his extreme distaste for drinking men, Moffett had declared that he would rather be subject to "good Negro rule" than to that of "the alcoholic devil." This statement drew a "swift and pointed" response from local Democratic newspapers. For white Democrats, such language recalled the outraged assertion that they themselves had made only six years earlier that Southside Virginia was, in fact, under the rule of Negro officeholders. During a brief period after the Civil War, blacks and whites in Virginia and elsewhere in the South had formed coalition governments. In Virginia, the Readjuster Party had given blacks their first opportunity to participate in state and local government as officeholders and appointees. This ended when a race riot erupted in Danville in 1883.[1]

Although they had regained control of the state, white Democrats in the late 1880s remained uneasy. Prohibitionists such as Reverend Moffett were perceived by the Democratic Party as threats to its political agenda. Moffett and his fellow prohibitionists deepened the divide between "wets" (drinkers) and "drys" (nondrinkers) and thereby threatened the white solidarity necessary to achieve Democratic rule and white dominance of social and political institutions.

In 1891, the year before his death, Reverend Moffett had been involved in the election battle over local option in Danville. In an eerie foreshadowing of his later encounter with Clark, Moffett experienced a close call when a man put a pistol against Moffett's chest and pulled the trigger. The gun misfired and Moffett was unharmed. In the election, the city of Danville went "wet" by eighteen votes, but Moffett continued to agitate for prohibition.

In October 1892, Moffett preached a prohibition sermon in which he argued that solving the liquor problem would also solve the so-called Negro problem.[2] Moffett asserted that liquor was the root cause of the difficulties between blacks and whites, as well as black crime and corrupt voting by blacks. But Moffett himself was accused of corruption when he tried to subvert the procedure that required voters to obtain tickets from ticket holders at the polls (and thereby reveal how they intended to vote). Moffett attempted to distribute Democratic tickets in the community, but because of what he described as an error by the printer, he ended up handing out bogus tickets. When J.T. Clark encountered Moffett on the street, he accused him of fraud. Enraged, Moffett struck Clark. Moffett also accidentally struck a police officer who attempted to intervene. Both he and Clark were arrested and fined.[3]

In an attempt to defend his reputation, Moffett went to the local newspaper, the *Danville Register*, and placed a "card" (a public statement). Moffett's defense of his honor appeared in the *Register* the day after he was shot by Clark. Earlier, in his own prohibitionist newspaper, Moffett had lashed out at Clark, calling him a "one-horse lawyer" and expressing his contempt for him. Although it was true that he had no law office, Clark did attempt to use the legal system against Moffett. Before the shooting, Clark had sought advice from two other attorneys. These two lawyers later represented Clark, but they were not in their offices on the day he went in search of them. The lawyer Clark did speak to would later prosecute Clark for Moffett's murder.

Clark had been out of town when Moffett's newspaper came out with the attack on his character. When he returned to Danville and to his work for the Democratic Party, Clark was praised by party members for his stance against Moffett. Later he learned about the article concerning him in Moffett's newspaper. He apparently went about town looking for a copy. He saw Moffett in the print shop office and left. But the two men met in the street, and a scuffle ensued. Four shots were fired. Moffett was hit in the abdomen by one of the bullets. The chief of police and a prominent citizen witnessed the encounter and rushed to restrain Clark. Both Moffett and Clark were arrested. Clark was taken to jail; Moffett was taken to a doctor.[4]

The downfall of a political enemy was celebrated by some local Democrats. Other Democrats, including the editor of the *Register*, rallied to Moffett's bedside. At this point, Moffett was at the mercy of late nineteenth-century medicine. The attending physicians opened his abdomen, looking for the bullet. They took out his intestines and ran them through their hands. Unable to find the bullet, the physicians sewed him up, even though they thought that he was bleeding from the liver. Moffett, who had been given chloroform, was revived with an enema of whiskey mixed with strychnine. When Moffett regained consciousness, he was informed that he was going to die. Indeed, he was dead within twenty-four hours after he had been shot by Clark. His death probably was attributable to both the shock and trauma of the bullet wound and an infection from the operation to repair the damage.[5]

Before he died, Moffett was visited by the mayor of Danville. He spoke to the mayor and other officials and to the friends who had gathered. He made a dying declaration in which he said that his nemesis, J.T. Clark, had shot him without warning.[6]

Even though a minister had been shot by a politician, the case did not receive widespread coverage by the media. A New York prohibition newspaper, the *Voice*, asserted that there was little chance that Moffett would receive justice. The Virginia Baptists, who viewed Moffett as a martyr to the prohibition cause, shared this sentiment. However, the Democratic newspapers portrayed the shooting as a private affair, unrelated to the prohibition fight.

In February 1893, Clark went to trial before Judge Archer Aiken. He was represented by five of Danville's best lawyers. Since Clark was not wealthy, it is possible that the Democratic Party paid for his defense. On the other side, the prosecutor of the case had been in office less than a year. A member of the Democrat machine, he was conducting his first big trial. He was joined at the prosecution table by a lawyer from outside the city who was being promoted as a candidate for lieutenant governor. In addition to this lawyer, Moffett's brother joined the team. However, the prosecutor resisted the attempts by out-of-state prohibition lawyers offering their assistance as well.

Because political feeling surrounding the case was strong, it was difficult finding jurors. Finally, one Danville man and eleven from Lynchburg were seated as the jury. As might have been expected, Clark claimed that he had acted in self-defense. His attorneys focused on the attack by Moffett, the editor of a newspaper, on Clark's honor. Clark's lawyers also blamed Moffett's doctors for their part in the minister's demise. On the other side, the prosecution argued that Clark had cold-bloodedly killed his nemesis. Those who believed that Clark had been a part of a conspiracy claimed that Clark, who the prohibitionists alleged was an ex-barkeeper, had acted as a tool of the whiskey ring.

However, rather than viewing Clark as a part of a political conspiracy, the jury apparently gave some credence to his assertion—one of five lines of defense offered by his attorneys—that he had acted in self-defense when he shot Moffett. To the outrage of the Moffett family and the prohibitionists, Clark was found guilty of voluntary manslaughter rather than first-degree murder. However, Clark's appeal of his five-year sentence failed.[7]

Virginia newspapers had treated the Danville trial as a human interest story rather than a political saga.[8] However, the case highlighted the multiple threads of a debate about alcohol that involved not only politics but also religion and race relations. It was not until the turn of the century, with black disenfranchisement, that the tensions would lessen between prohibitionists and those who were focused on achieving white political solidarity.

By the turn of the century, Danville had attracted notice as an Old South tobacco town that was now moving aggressively to become a New South industrial phenomenon. To understand Danville in the early twentieth century requires a look back at Danville's history.

FROM TRADING POST TO MILL TOWN

Laid out along the banks of a river, Danville, like other cumulative communities, drew its settlers from other areas. The area was surveyed by Colonel William Byrd of Westover Plantation during a 1728 exploration to establish the exact boundary line between Virginia and North Carolina. Byrd gave the territory the name "Dan" from a Biblical passage referring to "from Dan to Beersheba." Ten years later, William Wynne purchased two hundred acres on the south side of the Dan River and later moved his family into this new country. The settlement was known as Wynne's Falls. Shortly after the Revolutionary War, war-impoverished families from the eastern part of Virginia migrated to the sparsely settled area.[9]

In 1793, a tobacco warehouse was established at Wynne's Falls, and the name of the settlement was changed to Danville. Danville was established as a town by an act of the Virginia legislature. This action by the legislature was, at least in part, a response to the need for further commercial development of the site. After John Barnett, the owner of the land on the south side of the river, established a ferry operation, trade in the settlement increased.[10]

The evolution of Danville from settlement to city paralleled the growth of Lynchburg and other, older cities in the area. In the Piedmont region of the state, where Danville is located, tobacco was one of the most important staple crops both in terms of farming and of factories. In fact, tobacco grew better in Piedmont Virginia than did some other crops. The tobacco growers relied on the labor of black slaves. Because of this, African Americans were heavily involved in the tobacco industry in the area from the beginning. In fact, a slave is supposed to have accidentally discovered how to consistently produce the bright-leafed tobacco for which the area became famous.

However, it was the planters who wanted to make Danville the market to which farmers in surrounding areas brought their tobacco. They obtained an inspection station in Danville. Then, in 1858, Thomas D. Neal (perfecting an idea of Dr. Stovall of Halifax County) began to display tobacco on the warehouse floor rather than in hogsheads (barrels). This method became associated with the city as the "Danville system." The system allowed buyers to see what they were purchasing. The system also provided farmers with higher prices for their tobacco than when it was sold by the hogshead.[11]

View of the Rebel hospitals, Danville. *Courtesy Library of Congress.*

Former tobacco factory and site of Confederate Prison No. 6, Danville. *Photo by Alice Green.*

Historic marker of Confederate Prison No. 6, Danville. *Photo by Alice Green.*

In 1862, during the Civil War, Danville "became a medical center for sick and wounded soldiers. Most of the hospital buildings were converted tobacco warehouses."[12] Danville also served as a prison exchange center. Six tobacco warehouses in Danville were used as stockades for Union prisoners. Nearly 7,000 prisoners were held in Danville, and more than 3,500 prisoners "died from cold, dysentery, and small pox."[13] The high death rates of prisoners in camps north and south could also be attributed to the harsh treatment that was prevalent in prison camps during the war.[14]

No battles of the Civil War were ever fought within the corporate limits of the city, but when the war began Danville was well positioned to play an important role. By 1856, the 140 miles of the Richmond and Danville Railroad had been completed. The railroad linked Danville to the state capital, and that would give Danville a crucial role to play during the war as a part of the Confederate supply line. At the same time, local newspapers had access to wire service and began to adopt a modern style of reporting.[15]

At the end of the war, in April 1865, when Jefferson Davis retreated from Richmond, he stopped in Danville. He stayed at the mansion of William T. Sutherlin, a prominent tobacco factory owner and quartermaster of Danville. During that week (April 3–10), Davis convened his cabinet. Thus,

Historic marker of site of last Confederate capitol, Danville. *Photo by Alice Green.*

Danville Museum, former Sutherlin Mansion, site of last Confederate capitol. *Photo by Alice Green.*

the Danville building gained its place in Civil War history as the "Last Capitol of the Confederacy."[16] However, the correspondence of leading Danville citizens with federal officials indicates that the city fathers were equally gratified by the reputation for hospitality that Danville had acquired in its reception of the Union army of occupation.[17]

One of the most dramatic events to occur in Danville happened between April 11 and April 17. As civilians and soldiers flocked to Danville seeking food and other supplies, there was looting and increasing concern that the city would not be able to maintain order. An explosion at the Confederate arsenal located a few hundred yards from the depot in Danville (perhaps at the end of Craghead Street) resulted in at least fourteen deaths. The explosion also sent the would-be looters fleeing from the city because they believed that the Yankees were attacking.[18]

With the rest of Virginia, Danville escaped the prolonged period of Radical Reconstruction experienced by states in the lower South. By 1869, the control of the government of Virginia had reverted to Bourbon Democratic hands. But the period following the Civil War was marked by an unparalleled participation by blacks, many of them former slaves, in politics and government.[19] White concern about black political participation increased when William Mahone, a self-made railroad tycoon, formed a third party in the state. This party, the Readjusters, attempted to challenge Bourbon Democratic rule in Virginia. It brought together all those who were dissatisfied with the manner in which the Democrats were handling the debt that the state shared with West Virginia, the railroad tariffs, education and other issues.

The leadership of the Readjuster Party—for reasons of political expediency—encouraged and sought black participation.[20] Between 1879 and 1883, the Readjusters established themselves on both the state and the national level and gained control over the federal patronage offices in the state. In 1879, the Readjusters had drawn support from the predominantly African American "Black Belt" counties of the Southside, including Danville. Some blacks were elected to local or to state political office—most of them to lower-echelon positions.[21]

In 1883, as the November General Assembly election approached, the Democrats made the fact that blacks were sitting in the state legislature and participating in county and municipal governments a campaign issue. White

Main Street, Danville, circa 1914. *Courtesy Clara Fountain.*

Dudley Block, Main Street, Danville, circa 1910. *Courtesy Clara Fountain.*

voters were urged to unite behind the Democratic Party and its slate of candidates in order to end the threat of black rule.

According to the Democrats, the threat of Negro rule had already become a reality in Danville. As Election Eve 1883 approached, the Democrats made speeches and issued flyers in which they described the situation in Danville as illustrative of the manner in which blacks and their white political allies were taking over the state. In Danville, the population was more than 50 percent black, but whites paid more than 90 percent of the city's taxes. White Democrats also were not happy with what they characterized as black dominance of municipal positions.[22] In terms of numbers, the Readjuststers' "black and tan" coalition had won seven of twelve city council seats in the 1882 election, and a white Readjuster, J.B. Raulston, was serving at the president of the council. Four of the councilmen were black. There was one black justice of the peace. Four of nine vacancies on the police department had been filled by blacks. Black men had been appointed to the positions of health officer and of weight master of the public scales.[23]

The presence of these black men in city government was the primary focus of the Danville Circular of 1883. The signers of the circular were "merchants and manufacturers and mechanics of the town of Danville."[24] Some of these men were prominent members of the commercial-civic elite well into the twentieth century. In 1883, these signers of the circular asserted that Danville was suffering economically as well as socially because of the racial climate in the city. Farmers, they said, were bringing their tobacco crops to the market in Durham, North Carolina, rather than sell in Danville. The Police Court, the circular asserted, was "another scene of perpetual mockery and disgrace." The most active of the magistrates was a black man named Jones, "who first became famous by seducing a girl under promise of marriage." According to the circular, in the Danville Police Court there was "malice and partiality, whenever there is motive, and ignorance in its absence." White men were allegedly arrested for the "most frivolous acts by negro policemen and borne along to the Mayor's office followed by swarms of jeering and hooting and mocking negroes."[25]

The tension between blacks and whites in Danville had been heightened by an incident that summer in which three black highwaymen allegedly attacked a young white farmer and his son as they were returning to their

Abe Koplen Clothing, established in the 1880s, North Union Street, Danville. *Photo by Alice Green.*

home from the city. During the robbery, the farmer was killed. Mob violence in Danville was only averted by the removal of the three black men from the city. They were later tried and executed.[26] This episode, coupled with what many whites in the city perceived as the arrogance and rudeness of former slaves (who no longer observed antebellum racial etiquette), contributed to the erosion of the racial situation in the community. The arrival of a prominent white Readjuster named William Sims for a round of speechmaking on the Friday afternoon before the Tuesday election set the stage for what followed.[27]

The spark that ignited the Danville Riot of 1883 came on that Saturday afternoon in November in the form of a minor sidewalk incident. The city was bustling with shoppers, people getting off from work and others attending political rallies. The Democrats were holding a mass meeting. Outside, a young black man bumped into a young white man on the sidewalk. The white man went on to the Democratic rally. But later, he left the rally and returned to the street, where he and a friend became involved in a brawl with the black man and two of his friends. Before the confrontation was over, armed whites had taken to the streets and were firing upon unarmed blacks. Blacks retreated to the black neighborhoods of the town. By evening, a tense calm had settled over the city as local white militia patrolled the streets.

The *New York Times* described the riot as the "Danville Fracas."[28] The riot shattered the Readjuster coalition. In the Tuesday election, many whites returned to the Democratic fold, and many blacks in Danville and elsewhere stayed away from the polls.[29] Although the threat of black rule in the state was now an empty one, black political participation remained an issue in Virginia until the majority of African Americans were disenfranchised by the Constitutional Convention of 1901–2. Long before this, with the Riot of 1883, Danville had returned to its racial status quo. Control of the city government reverted to white Democratic hands, and the business leaders of the city turned their attention to economic progress and industrialization.[30]

Starting a cotton mill was one of the priorities of men such as J.H. Schoolfield (one of the signers of the Danville Circular). As the biographer of Schoolfield's brother, Robert, explains, most jobs associated with the tobacco business were "menial, low-paid, and sometimes sporadic" and therefore considered "unsuitable for whites." Blacks were actively recruited to do these jobs.[31] A new industry was deemed necessary not only to boost the economy of the city but also to supply more jobs for white laborers. One of the problems encountered by the owners of the Dan River and Riverside Cotton Mills was how to obtain and keep their workers. The solution was

Danville messengers. Western Union No. 5, Danville. *Courtesy Library of Congress.*

View looking southwest, 220 Newton Street, constructed circa 1915. *Courtesy Library of Congress.*

stepped-up recruitment and the construction of a mill village of tenant houses known as "Schoolfield Village."[32] The Village lay outside Danville corporate limits and was autonomous. Robert Schoolfield, who was one of the supporters of the temperance movement in Danville, prohibited the consumption of alcoholic beverages in the Village itself.[33]

The mills were a significant economic boost to the Danville community. An important political factor in the life of the city was the fact that men such as the Schoolfield brothers, their associates and several prominent tobacco warehousemen served lengthy tenures in public office. As one contemporary writer of the period explained: "The people of Danville do not take much stock in rotation in office. When they get a good man, they like to keep him."[34] What this meant, however, was that these business and industrial leaders came to make up a commercial-civic elite in the city.

For better or worse, this elite exerted influence over all of the institutions in the city of Danville, including the criminal justice system. However, there were other influences that would also come into play during the era examined in this book. The legacy of slavery in the South would continue to shape the relations between blacks and whites long after the last gun had been fired in the War Between the States. Temperance, as a national movement, gained momentum during the late nineteenth and early twentieth centuries. Progressive Era reformers attempted to bring about a variety of changes in society. At the same time, xenophobia and the fear of radical politics reached new heights during the decade following World War I. Urbanization, industrialization and the production of new consumer products, including radios and cars, would all play a role in shaping the nation—and Danville. So would churches and baseball teams and movies. Danville did not exist in isolation. But the forces that shaped American society would shape Danville in ways that were unique to the city.

CHAPTER 2

The Commercial-Civic Elite

Business and Politics

By the early twentieth century, the "psychological fabric of a good community"[35] existed in Danville, but it was a community in which commerce vied with tradition. A number of prominent business and professional men were not natives of the city. They had migrated there from other cities in Virginia or from North Carolina or other parts of the South. Once settled, these men married, started families, founded businesses and became involved in city government. Simpson notes in his 1891 account of *Men, Places and Things in Danville* that the city began as "an aggregate of incongruous elements, each intent upon the pursuit of his own pet project for making money, and making it rapidly."[36]

The most important industries in Danville were the cotton mills and the tobacco factories. In its first issue in January 1905, the *Danville Register* reported that the sale of tobacco for the past twelve months had been unprecedented. Danville, according to the newspaper, was the "world's leading bright leaf tobacco market," handling 45 million pounds per annum at a value of $3.5 million.[37] The president of the Danville Tobacco Association, E.G. Moseley, was also a prominent member of the city council. In 1905, Moseley proposed a stronger liquor ordinance. In 1922, he was a member of the Law and Order League, whose chief goal was the enforcement of prohibition.

In the same 1905 article on the city's progress, the *Register* noted that the new mill had been completed and that a new village with "several thousand inhabitants" had sprung up around it in the "suburbs of the city."[38] The Riverside Cotton Mills had been founded in July 1882 by Thomas B.

House in "Millionaire's Row," Main Street, Danville. *Photo by Alice Green.*

Houses in "Millionaire's Row," Main Street, Danville. *Photo by Alice Green.*

Fitzgerald, the first president, Dr. H.W. Cole, Benjamin F. Jefferson, and the three Schoolfield brothers, John, James and Robert Addison.[39]

Later, the Riverside Cotton Mills was merged with the Morotock Mills, and in 1895, the mill owners chartered a separate company, the Dan River Power and Manufacturing Company, to develop water power in the Dan River. In 1926, the cotton mills represented the leading industry in the city with 5,672 employees. About 90 percent of the mill employees were white. The blacks who worked at the mills held unskilled positions such as water boys or loaders.[40] As its founders had intended, the mills provided jobs for white workers.

Like E.G. Moseley, John Schoolfield was a member of the Anti-Saloon League. In 1905, Schoolfield and Moseley were both delegates to the state convention in Lynchburg. Schoolfield agreed with Moseley that a stiffer penalty for public drunkenness in the city of Danville should be enacted—as Moseley put it, the one-dollar fine in effect in 1905 was a "farce."[41] John Schoolfield's support of the temperance cause might be explained by the fact that he and his brothers were the sons of a Methodist minister. All of the Schoolfield brothers appear to have been church workers. James, like John,

Noon hour at Riverside Cotton Mills, Danville, June 2, 1911. *Courtesy Library of Congress.*

A couple of dinner-toters at Riverside Cotton Mills, Danville. *Courtesy Library of Congress.*

View looking south of 656 Monument Street, built circa 1898 as John T. Luther's grocery. *Courtesy Library of Congress.*

was involved in the temperance movement. He also served the city in various civic capacities. However, after one term as Danville's representative in the state legislature, he declined renomination because he found that "politics was not congenial to him."[42]

Commenting on the influence exerted by certain men in the city over the local government, a contemporary raconteur, writer and sometime politician, Harry Ficklen, suggested that in Danville there existed an "invisible government." Ficklen charged that the city failed to move forward as it should because of "an anonymous oligarchy—an invisible government composed of thoroughly good men." According to Ficklen, these men were associated with the Riverside and Dan River Cotton Mills, and they prevented the expansion of Danville to incorporate Schoolfield Village. He went on to charge that this invisible government used religious organizations and women to reach its ends.[43]

In fact, in 1920, the Young Men's Business Association had joined with the chamber of commerce to create the Good Government Club. The club put forth a resolution to change what it described as the outmoded bicameral structure of municipal government and to replace it with a smaller single

Dan River Mills building, Schoolfield, now closed. *Photo by Alice Green.*

body. The club argued that businessmen should handle the business of the city, speaking here of the new business class who belonged to the chamber of commerce and played golf, not the small merchants of Danville. With rallies, ads and boosterism, the club deflected the arguments made by those who favored the old ward system. Among the opponents of the change were working-class men of North Danville (some of them millworkers), who were concerned about power being "centralized" in the hands of the elite. The citizens of Danville voted in favor of the new council structure. Subsequently, the Good Government Club offered its own slate of candidates. For the next twenty years, until after World War II, businessmen from this group won elections and ran city government.[44]

Until 1950, when the power of the Good Government Club waned and Danville finally sued for annexation, Schoolfield Village remained autonomous. The executives of the mills set the rules and regulations by which the workers who lived in the Village were required to abide by. Yet in spite of the Schoolfields' attitude toward drinking and the banning of alcohol in Schoolfield Village, the millworkers still drank and engaged in drunken fights and brawls, which created law enforcement problems for the Danville police. Perhaps this was one of the reasons why the Riverside Cotton Mills executives were so persistent in their efforts to see antiliquor laws enacted and enforced in Danville. It should be noted that the wives of these men were also active. In 1922, for example, Mrs. Fitzgerald was president of the Woman's Christian Temperance Union (WCTU) in Danville. She was of the opinion that Mayor Harry Wooding, who was also the lower court magistrate, was too lenient in the penalties that he imposed on the prohibition violators brought before him.[45]

According to accounts of his life, Mayor Wooding had gained the respect of white Democrats when he "carried a gun" during the Riot of 1883.[46] Wooding had been a seventeen-year-old private in the Confederate army. He entered politics in Danville as a city councilman, replacing one of the councilmen who had resigned after the riot. For the next four decades, he would be a fixture in Danville politics, until he died in office at the age of ninety-three.

Mayor Wooding was a stumbling block to those who advocated a dry Danville. In 1905, when Schoolfield and Moseley proposed a stiffer penalty for public drunkenness, Wooding, who had some discretion in the matter of imposing fines, "intimated that he did not think the matter wise legislation." He is reported to have observed that "in all his long life he had never known a reformed drunkard except through the grace of God." According to the mayor, it was not possible to "legislate goodness and morality into a man's heart." He felt that the stiffer penalty "would be taking the bread out of the mouths of babes."[47] What existed in Danville was a division along proliquor and antiliquor lines ("wets" and "drys"). Mayor Wooding, although apparently not known as a drinker, carried the votes of the wets because of his views on the enforcement of the liquor laws. At the same time, there was a dry faction made up of members of the commercial-civic leadership in Danville.

In Danville, as elsewhere in the country, the crusade against liquor may have provided blacks with one means of obtaining social status and aligning themselves

Statue of Mayor Harry Wooding in front of the Danville Courthouse. *Photo by Alice Green.*

with the white community's elite. For blacks, as for whites, advocating temperance was a declaration of commitment to Protestantism, the work ethic and the status quo. In 1909, the Negro Anti-Saloon League closed its three-day convention in Atlanta, Georgia, by adopting a resolution acknowledging the "splendid movement now being carried forward by our white neighbors for prohibition." The Atlanta convention added: "We recognize that the saloon has been the cause of the greatest part of crime committed by the weaker element of our race."[48] When Mrs. Amy Weeher, the state organizer of the Virginia WCTU, came to Danville, she gave an address to the black community at High Street Baptist Church, one of the two churches to which most of the members of the black commercial-civic elite belonged.[49] Therefore, it may be assumed that some blacks in Danville did have an interest in and were participating in the temperance movement.

However, black opinion about the matter was not of any great weight or political importance according to the *Danville Register*. In an editorial response to an editorial by the *Roanoke Times*, another Virginia newspaper, the *Register* asserted that "the Negro bugaboo should scare nobody." As the Danville newspaper assessed the situation, if the officers of registration and election would "do their duty honestly, few Negroes will be able to vote." According to the *Register*, those blacks still qualified to vote under properly enforced laws would favor prohibition.[50] Perhaps the *Register* based its prediction on the link between the temperance movement and the Protestant church. Most blacks who met the qualifications for voters were also members of the upper and middle classes and were churchgoers. Or perhaps the *Register* was implying that the blacks who could vote had a vested interest in aligning themselves with the "safe" position of antiliquor.

At any rate, in Danville, the purity of the temperance movement in differentiating class status, at least among whites, was not absolute. The mayor's stance on the issue has already been discussed. In May 1914, Rorer A. James, the editor of the *Danville Register* who became chairman of the state Democratic Party in 1916, ordered sixteen gallons of whiskey before the statewide referendum on prohibition. He is reported to have said: "I believe in looking ahead. I don't know what the pro-hibs will do in September, but I do not mean for them to catch me high and dry in any event."[51]

It was James's newspaper that brought the local news of the temperance crusade to the people of Danville. James had purchased the newspaper at auction in 1899 and reestablished the paper's fallen circulation. In 1921, when James died, his son, Rorer James Jr., took over the newspaper and continued the policies of his father.[52] One of these policies was to view the conflict between "wets" and "drys" in Danville as a political controversy. Clearly, in Danville some members of the commercial-civic elite were anti-prohibition or "personally wet"—or, at least, not as conservative as the temperance forces might have wished them to be in their views.

In Virginia, the temperance movement cannot be isolated from the churches that served as its base. The movement in Virginia was led by James Cannon Jr., a Methodist minister, who became the directing head of the Anti-Saloon League in 1904. The Virginia Anti-Saloon League "worked closely with the national organization and benefited from its experience,"[53] but it also possessed a flavor that was characteristic of the Old Dominion. Cannon, the Virginia superintendent of the league, manipulated the famous (or infamous) Democratic machine. In Virginia, liquor "was outlawed by the alliance between the moral forces and the most conservative political organization in any southern state."[54] Cannon and his church workers in cities like Danville created a political organization, the Anti-Saloon League, through which the moral forces of temperance could exercise their political influence. It was "the church in action against the saloons."[55] Throughout the state, politicians sometimes found it expedient to side with the dry forces.

In the early twentieth century, prohibition came to Virginia with the political support of the Democratic organization. How many of the machine leaders were personally for it or voted for it on election day can never be known. During each of the campaigns against the saloon, there were references to leaders who were politically dry and personally wet. While they liked their whiskey and may have doubted the wisdom of prohibition, they deemed it politically expedient to side with the dry cause.[56]

In Danville, Mayor Wooding appears to have either believed in candor or to have felt that his political base was secure enough to withstand the disapproval of the prohibitionists. In each election, he received consistent support from the "wets" and enough support from other Danville citizens to carry every mayoral contest from 1892 until his death in 1938.

In 1924, Wooding won by the very narrowest of margins: one vote. His opponent, Charles K. Carter, the president of the Danville Automotive Association and the proprietor of the Dan Valley Motor Company, had promised and apparently conducted a quiet, dignified campaign. He and Wooding avoided a runoff election by the equally dignified strategy of separating the offices of mayor and lower court magistrate. Although there was passing discussion about the legality of this step, Carter became the magistrate of what had been known as Mayor's Court, and the office of Police Court justice was finally created in Danville.

COVERING DANVILLE'S BLACK ELITE

Being a part of the temperance movement was only one form of commitment made by blacks who aspired to middle- and upper-class status. The black entrepreneurial class in southern cities shared many of the goals and attitudes of its white counterpart.[57] The views and opinions of the black elite permeated the majority of black newspapers and journals published during the period. The elite attempted to instruct other classes of blacks as to how to live moral and industrious lives.[58]

In Danville, there was no black newspaper. However, the black elite of Danville maintained close ties with a black newspaper, the *Richmond Planet*, and its editor, John Mitchell Jr. "[A]mong the state's most influential black men,"[59] Mitchell published a weekly column recounting his travels throughout the state, and there were frequent references to the hospitality that he had received from his friends in Danville. The *Planet* also had an agent and local, although unnamed, contributors in Danville. Its descriptions of Danville's black society weddings, anniversaries, fetes and entertainments, as well as cultural events, were read by the black community in Danville. Blacks in Danville were informed, for example, that "the home of Reverend and Mrs. R.G. Adams was the social Mecca for Danville's black society on Wednesday evening,"[60] that "Mrs. Minnie Moton Reed owned a handsome automobile"[61] or that the reading room at the Owl Club "would make the manager of any Richmond club step aside with envy."[62] The *Planet* carried the news of Danville's black baseball team and of the travels of its black citizens. The *Planet* also carried items on acts of generosity by members of the elite, such as restaurant owner George Rison, who on Christmas Day fed the black poor and, during World War I, saw black soldiers off with farewell dinners. It reported as well that "Mr. J.R. Wilson of Danville, Virginia won a notable victory in Chicago when he succeed in getting seated over the heads of the 'lily white' contingent" of the Virginia Republican Party.[63]

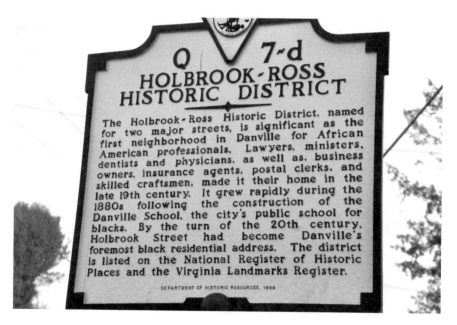

Historic marker of Holbrook-Ross district, an African American neighborhood. *Photo by Alice Green.*

First State Bank, African American owned/operated, North Union Street, Danville. *Photo by Alice Green.*

The newspaper reported the activities of the Federation of Colored Women's Clubs in Danville and of the Virginia State Baptist convention the several times it met in the city. The Knights of Pythias, a black lodge, received special attention because John Mitchell was one of the ranking state officers and reported on the activities of all of the lodge courts throughout the state. When the National Association for the Advancement of Colored People (NAACP) was organized in Danville in 1918, the *Planet* reported that the Danville branch of the NAACP had been organized on February 12 with forty-five charter members.[64] A month later, it reported the successful intervention in a court case by NAACP officers and some of Danville's "best white citizens," who had crowded Mayor Wooding's courtroom to see that justice was done in the case of a black man who had been unjustly charged by a police officer.[65]

In its letters-to-the-editor column, the *Planet* provided Danville black leaders with one forum for expressing their views about issues of the day. Attorney Carter, a black Danville lawyer, used it to ask a "vital question" during World War I about why there was "all this hullabaloo about the loyalty of the Negro to the American flag?"[66]

In the 1920s, the *Planet* covered the revival of the Ku Klux Klan (KKK) in Danville and elsewhere in the state just as it had reported on the Jim Crow laws and their effect on black citizens of Virginia. Understandably, the *Planet* took an anti-lynching stance. Clearly, although Danville blacks did not have a newspaper of their own, they did have a newspaper available for the dissemination of information about and to the community.

BLACK RACIAL PROGRESS

In 1902, a visiting black minister who had preached at both High Street and Loyal Baptist, the churches attended by the black elite, was impressed by the "colored citizens of Danville." He found them energetic, thrifty and progressive and noted that "[t]hey believe in the Negro doing for himself and this is seen by them being largely engaged in business of various kinds."[67]

In December 1909, the *Danville Register* carried the obituary of Robert J. Adams, age sixty, "[o]ne of the most widely known colored citizens of Danville." The newspaper noted that after the Civil War Adams had been "a member of the local police force when the city was under Negro domination." At the time of his death, Adams owned a barbershop on Craghead Street (and lived in the house in the rear). He was also involved in a transfer business and led a "colored orchestra." He was a member of High Street Baptist Church and the colored lodges of the Masons and Uniform Rank Knight of Pythias. A Danville native, Adams "was regarded as one of the leaders among his race, and had many friends, both among the white and colored residents of the city."[68] In spite of Adams's brief tenure as a policeman, he was obviously accepted by whites as a respectable member of the black community.

High Street Baptist Church, Danville. *Photo by Alice Green.*

ERECTED 1873
BURNED 1878
REBUILT 1878
BURNED 1901
REBUILT 1901

STORM DAMAGE
JUNE 8, 1995
RESTORATION COMPLETED
NOVEMBER 22, 1995

Cornerstone of High Street Baptist Church, Danville. *Photo by Alice Green.*

In Danville, there was a black savings, loan and investment association. There were black teachers, lawyers, doctors, restaurant owners and undertakers. In 1904, Editor Mitchell of the *Richmond Planet* reported that Holbrook and Cunningham, the black undertakers, had a "new funeral car and a fine rubber tired carriage."[69] In 1911, the *Planet* reported that Mr. Cunningham, who hailed from Manchester, Virginia, "is now the most popular undertaker and embalmer in the city of Danville, being highly respected by both white and colored people."[70] However, another local black undertaker suffered "an ugly moment" after a 1917 lynching of a black man. The undertaker mounted a fire wagon to convey a message to a Danville policeman, and an angry crowd of white citizens mistook his intentions. The "irate citizens" thought that he was trying to "save the remains" of the dead man. They "mobbed" the undertaker, who fled headlong before the crowd of pursuers. Finally, he sank under a rain of blows. His coat was cut, but he was protected from further violence by the police.[71]

This episode highlights an important fact about black life in Danville and the rest of the South during this era. Even though the members of the black elite—and other blacks who were chosen to be the recipients of white patronage—might have occupied a protected position in the community with regard to routine law enforcement activities, in a moment of crisis, of intense emotion, even those blacks who were protected by their class, occupation, or white "friends" might find themselves at risk because they possessed a black face. This, of course, was one of the reasons the black elite had a vested interest in keeping the peace in Danville. Every episode of black-white violence threatened their own fragile status position. This status position was one that they occupied within a caste system.

The boundaries that separated blacks and whites were physical and geographical as well as social. The Supreme Court decision in *Plessy v. Ferguson* (1896) had affirmed the concept of "separate but equal" public accommodations. In the South, Jim Crow laws had established racial segregation on public transportation and in public facilities such as restaurants, train depots, theaters and parks. The most far-reaching of these laws were enacted in the 1920s and 1930s, but as early as 1906, a Jim Crow streetcar law was pending before the Virginia state legislature. The *Danville Register* observed that this law had been in effect in Richmond for several years and had worked there. The newspaper added that the "Negroes of Danville Object to Jim Crow Law Less Than Any Others." The *Register* claimed that the black people of Danville had accepted the law with little effort to show any displeasure. Unlike blacks in other Virginia cities who had staged boycotts and protests, blacks in Danville had become used to the new arrangement and were responding to it in "a most satisfactory way." They should, according to the *Register*, be "congratulated on the sensible view taken on the matter, and law abiding and peaceable way in which they acted."[72]

In 1900, the *Richmond Planet* had observed with regard to the railroads that the Jim Crow laws were rebounding to the "benefit of blacks and discomfort of whites" because whites were compelled to obey the law, too, and because blacks now found themselves with private rail cars. The *Planet* said that black people had decided to "yield an unwilling acquiescence to the law and those who expected trouble would find themselves keenly disappointed."[73]

Apparently, this stance of not resisting the segregation laws and avoiding trouble was one that blacks in Danville continued to abide by even when blacks in some other Virginia cities, including Richmond, had turned to protest. It should be pointed out that the *Register* supported the race position of Booker T. Washington, the African American leader who argued that blacks should focus on economic progress on their own side of the color line rather than seeking racial integration. The Danville newspaper found Washington's pragmatic conservatism preferable to what it perceived as the more radical view of the northern wing of the NAACP.

The *Register* was oddly silent about the NAACP in Danville. However, in 1917, the newspaper had carried a letter from black Danville leaders, "representative men of the race" who deplored a near riot between some young black men and white soldiers. In this letter, the black leaders cautioned the black citizens of Danville that during "these serious times" they should "season their utterances with soundest discretion" and offer their "heartiest cooperation" to white citizens.[74]

Undoubtedly, this was sound advice given the anti-seditionist spirit of the times. It was also an acknowledgement of some basic racial realities. By 1917, the year of both the near riot and the lynching, the physical boundaries between blacks and whites had been established. In 1915, the city council had enacted a residential segregation ordinance that made it unlawful for a white or a black person to establish residence "upon any street or alley between two adjacent streets on which a greater number of houses" were occupied by members of the other race.[75] Even earlier, certain sections of the city were recognized as black areas because of the numbers of blacks who lived there. These areas were often satellite communities on the outer edges of the city.

That same year, the blockbuster film *The Birth of a Nation* (1915) was released. Based on the novel *The Clansman* by ex-minister Thomas Dixon and directed by D.W. Griffith, the film told the tale of two white families caught up in the turmoil during and after the Civil War. With white actors in "blackface," the film presented the worst stereotypes of blacks during Reconstruction and reinforced the myth of the "black rapist." When the film arrived for a three-day engagement at the Majestic Theater in Danville, a delegation of fifty black citizens, "composed of ministers and the better class of colored citizenry," visited the mayor to ask that he prevent the showing of the film.

According to the *Register*, two black attorneys, W.P. Allen and John Carter, spoke to Mayor Wooding for half an hour. They presented their cause "deferentially but nevertheless ably." They asked that the film not be shown until a board of censors had reviewed it and determined that the "most objectionable features of the film be eliminated." However, after hearing them out, the mayor said that he would follow the precedent set by the mayors of Richmond and Norfolk, who had allowed the film to be shown without interference. He noted that there was no law under which he could prevent it from being shown. Even though Carter and Allen argued that the film represented "the Negro race in a light which is humiliating to the present generation" and was "calculated to cause a breach of the peace," Mayor Wooding assured them that he believed that the story presented was too far removed from the present to cause problems. He told them that the film had been shown in other cities with no trouble, in spite of the Richmond delegation that had protested the film.[76]

The images of blacks in the film paralleled the stereotypes often found in newspaper coverage. This was a period when newspapers across the South offered inflammatory descriptions of black criminality. But the characterization of black crime by the *Danville Register* was more conservative and less inflammatory than that of many lower South newspapers.[77] In fact, the *Register* often seems to have sought a middle ground in race relations, urging reason and good sense rather than what it considered the radical extremes of both left and right. The *Register* spoke out against both lynching by whites and activism by the NAACP. In the 1920s, this moderate stance by the newspaper was jeopardized by the resurgence of the Ku Klux Klan in Danville and briefly in 1921 by what the newspaper called a "black crime wave."

The Klan had been born in the aftermath of the Civil War, during the days of Reconstruction. The rebirth of the Klan in the aftermath of World War I was not universally welcomed by whites. A historian of the KKK writes:

> *The revival of the Deep South's cherished heroes of Reconstruction days was displeasing to many Virginians. In the spring of 1921, the Richmond chapter of the United Daughters of the Confederacy petitioned the governor to prevent the organization of the Klan in the state; the leaders of the Democratic party were never pro-Klan. The State Corporation Commission brought suit against the Klan and got it fined for carrying on unauthorized business in the state.*[78]

However, "[t]he centers of Klan strength in [Virginia] lay in a series of growing, industrialized cities." These cities included Norfolk, Newport News, Lynchburg, Roanoke—and Danville. Thus, "[h]undreds of Virginians packed Klan rallies in the Palace Theater in Danville."[79]

With regard to the Klan, the *Danville Register* carried reports of the efforts by blacks and by a city council member to prevent the proliferation of the nativist group by appealing to white church organizations. Yet it also accepted a full-page ad from the Klan in which the organization set forth its "American principles" in the Kreed of the KKK to which "Klansmen kneeling at the foot of the fiery cross have sworn allegiance."[80] The newspaper also provided coverage of the Klan's activities in the city, including its rallies in local churches and halls and a full-scale "naturalization ceremony" on a summer night during which Klansmen paraded one thousand strong through the main streets of the city.[81] Such coverage might be described as reasonable and understandable given the fact that the *Register*'s readers, both white and black, were interested in the Klan's activities. But when the *Register* referred to "another act of magnanimity" by the Klan in presenting a stranded traveler and his family with eighty dollars,[82] it is difficult to know if the newspaper is speaking with the proverbial tongue in cheek or as a supporter of at least some of the organization's activities.

This same ambiguity of tone is apparent in the *Register*'s coverage of the alleged "black crime wave" in 1921. On the front page of its Tuesday, March

1, 1921 issue, the newspaper reported that a black man who had attempted an attack on a white woman had been shot by her neighbor and that this was the climax of a series of offenses committed by blacks against whites since that Friday.[83] On the editorial page of the same issue, the newspaper demanded "a vigorous policy" in response to the crime wave sweeping the city that it saw as possibly explained by the fact that many were now idle and unwilling to work for reduced wages.

Without referring to black offenders, the *Register*, stating that it was not generally "inclined to an alarmist view," warned that "bloodshed [would] be unavoidable" if the crime wave did not "quickly and completely subside." This would happen, the newspaper asserted, because citizens were prone to mete out "swift, summary and vengeful punishment."[84]

The newspaper went on to note that the court was dealing with at least one offender but that hundreds of "ordinarily calm citizens" were still taking precautions to protect their homes and families. Yet the newspaper did at least appear to support a policy of nonviolence and moderation. It spoke out against both extralegal violence by citizens (lynchings) and excessive police violence in making arrests. The newspaper also gave printed support to the activities of interracial organizations that sought better race relations. In fact, in May, two months after it reported on the "black crime wave" (but before it began to report Klan activities), the newspaper expressed its regret in an editorial that the clergy of Danville had not followed the example of Roanoke, Virginia ministers who had appealed to the Roanoke City Council to maintain law and order. Receiving this appeal, the council in Roanoke had adopted a formal declaration that the city would do "without extraordinary aid." The *Register* noted that when Danville clergy had recently been asked to unite against "spectacular and unnecessary organizations, for which there is neither demand nor occasion," they had failed to do so. The *Register* asserted that such organizations would only "provoke racial feeling and distrust" when "the races here are and have long been peaceful, friendly and eminently satisfactory"[85]

The "organization" referred to in this editorial is the KKK. It appears that even though two months earlier the newspaper had perceived a "black crime wave" in the city, it did not find this recent rash of black offenses threatening enough to community stability to warrant organization by white Klansmen for defense against and control of blacks. The *Register* appears to have advocated vigorous action by the criminal justice system rather than by vigilante groups.

On the day following the May 12 editorial, the *Register* gave its support to the Virginia Commission for Interracial Cooperation, which as the newspaper noted was "designed not only to abate racial friction and promote better understanding in the South" but also to resist the "mischievous and pernicious" activities of the NAACP and provide a sane movement in the face of the revival of the Ku Klux Klan.[86] At its best, the newspaper appears to have been a force working to reduce tensions that threatened to result in outbreaks of racial violence, whether crime related or otherwise. At worst, the newspaper seems to have been blind to the state of race relations.

Perhaps even more indicative of the boundaries separating the black and white citizens of Danville was the lack of "moral" support from the source from which blacks had the most right to expect it. In 1921, when the Klan was reviving in Danville and in other cities throughout Virginia, the black ministers of Danville asked the white ministers of the Ministerial Union to aid them in stopping the proliferation of the KKK in the city. As noted by the *Register*, the white ministers considered the request from the black pastors— which "caused heated discussion"—but the request was "flatly turned down." Although the white ministers had decided not to talk about this discussion, the *Register* had it from a reliable source that the white ministers who favored aiding their black brethren had been overruled by those who questioned "what the result of such agitation would be." The ministers finally reached the expedient conclusion that although the new Klan had the same name as the old one and although the name "sounded deadly and recalled days immediately following the Civil War, in reality, the organization was similar to other fraternal bodies, and had no bad features."[87]

Two years later, in 1923, E.G. Mosely[88], "a lay delegate" from the Cabell Street Memorial Church, proposed a resolution condemning the Klan at a conference of the Danville District Methodist Episcopal Church. His resolution was defeated, and he was informed by the body that it was not the proper place for such a resolution.[89]

Mayor Wooding might welcome the representatives of the Virginia Baptist Convention to the city by giving a keynote address. The Danville Fair Association might set aside a day for blacks to display their exhibits during Fair Week. Certain blacks in the community might be described by the *Register* in favorable terms. But the boundary lines between blacks and whites were as clear as the see-no-evil message from the white Ministerial Union and the Methodist Episcopal Church. As a white mass meeting in Lynchburg had observed after the Danville Riot of 1883, "Negroes must know that they are to behave themselves and keep in their proper places."[90] To do otherwise was to discomfort some whites and threaten others.

CHAPTER 3

Public Order Crimes

During the early twentieth century, crusades against crime focused not only on violent crime but also on public order offenses (also known as "vice crimes"). During this Progressive Era, reformers ("moral entrepreneurs") formed organizations that attempted to influence both policymakers and the criminal justice process. The law violators who were the targets of these efforts were often perceived and described not only as disruptive but also as members of a "dangerous class" that threatened the public welfare.

On February 11, 1921, the *Danville Register* reported on its front page, "Grand Jury Probe Fails to Show City Lawless." The probe had come about after a local minister, Dr. Henry W. DuBose, preached a sermon in which he asserted that Danville was experiencing a crime wave. Judge D. Price Withers of Corporation Court charged a grand jury with investigating DuBose's assertions. During a two-day inquiry, the grand jury heard testimony from witnesses and informants. When it was done, the jury concluded that no indictments were justified. The main recommendation from the grand jury was that drugstores that were dispensing flavored extracts and patents medicines be warned about the use of these alcohol-containing concoctions as beverages.

The public, the *Register* noted, would be relieved that the inquiry had not produced the "appalling revelations" that everyone had anticipated. But the grand jury, made up of men who were business and civic leaders and church members, had not said that there was no crime in Danville.[91] Indeed, the *Register* itself was daily reporting on vice crimes and violence in Danville. In March 1921, the black United Ministers' Conference expressed its concern

about the crime wave "sweeping over our country, our state and our city."
The ministers presented themselves as ready "to affiliate with the white
people of Danville who are of our persuasion"—that is, white people who
want to "search for, expose, and suppress the brothels and dens of sensuality"
in the city.[92]

These reformers in Danville had some victories in their efforts to influence
the criminal justice system (as in the case of the grand jury investigation) but
were not successful in their efforts to abolish vice and other crime in the city.
As elsewhere when repressed, crime sometimes rebounded.

PUBLIC ORDER CRIMES AND TOLERATED DEVIANTS

There are some general statements that can be made about this category
of offenses. One is that these offenses were generally misdemeanors (except
for drug law violations and, later in the period, second-offense liquor law
violations). Because these offenses were misdemeanors, it might be argued
that the community had no choice but to tolerate such offenders. However,
there were other options available, and sometimes used, in Danville and
other cities that wished to be rid of certain types of offenders. For example,
the police could target individuals who were considered undesirable,
arresting them at every opportunity until eventually they either left town
or were sentenced on a more serious charge. Or the courts could offer an
offender a choice: "Leave town or go to jail." Most such offenders chose to
leave. In fact, the offender himself might offer to leave town if the charges
were dropped (an offer that was not always accepted).

As a second point to be made, in Danville public order convictions from
the lower courts were sometimes appealed to Corporation Court. This was
especially true in the case of liquor law violations, which made up the bulk
of the appeals. This is significant because in September 1924, C.K. Carter
became police justice, replacing Mayor Wooding as lower court magistrate.
Carter's handling of liquor law cases seems to have been more in keeping
with the repressive approach advocated by the antiliquor forces. However,
it should be noted that some offenders, particularly repeat offenders, seem
to have routinely filed an appeal of the lower court decision. Moreover,
Carter assumed the position of police justice five years after the Volstead
Act had established national prohibition and presumably would have had
more liquor law cases passing through his court. We must presume about
this because records are only available for the Corporation Court.

A third point about public order offenders is that the data provide some support for the assertion that some deviants were tolerated in the community. Based on a sample of the cases that appeared in Corporation Court (1900–1930), 270 individuals out of 1,798 were charged with two or more offenses during this period: 176 of these repeat offenders were black (157 male; 19 female), and 94 were white (90 male; 4 female). As a group, they appear in the newspaper and Corporation Court records as offenders who cycled in and out of the criminal justice system, being placed on bonds of good behavior, fined and jailed—but remaining in the community.[93]

A final point, the offenders could have been prosecuted under more than one statute for behavior that was a nuisance to the community. For example, the proprietor of a house that attracted a steady flow of loud, drunken visitors might have been charged under a 1907 ordinance with keeping a "disorderly house." The penalties were:

- Fine not more than $50.00, discretion of the mayor (as magistrate of Mayor's Court).
- Jail not less than five days, nor more than six months.
- Fine could be worked out a rate of 50 cents a day on streets or other public improvements.[94]

Liquor in Danville, 1900–1930

During the first three decades of the twentieth century, Danville was experiencing a "rural lag." The city had industrialized but had not lost its close ties to the countryside. In 1900, the population of Danville was 16,520. Thirty years later, in 1930, it was still only 22,247.[95] The citizens of Danville knew one another and engaged in face-to-face interactions. This meant that the members of the Anti-Saloon League and the Law and Order League were able to directly reach the members of the municipal government, their constituents and the offenders themselves. The Anti-Saloon League agitated for local option prohibition before the state enacted the Virginia Prohibition Act (the Mapp Act) in 1916. When national prohibition went into effect, these groups pushed for the enforcement of the liquor laws.

In 1905, Danville was dry. In January of that year, both the wets and the drys were mustering their forces for the local option election anticipated that summer. The adherents of each side were paying their poll taxes so that they would be qualified to vote. According to the *Register*, the "drys worked the hardest to rally their forces" because they were "determined, if possible, to maintain their supremacy." However, the "wets did good work too." As a result, both parties brought "many dollars in the tins of the collector and many electors qualified to vote."[96] Clearly, the issue of temperance affected other aspects of community life, such as the number of registered voters.

That January, the Anti-Saloon League criticized the police when it discovered that some local merchants had apparently purchased a federal license to distill liquor. The league obtained a list of these thirty-five merchants. Learning of this, Mayor Wooding and Chief of Police J.R. Ackers were "working hard to procure" a copy of the list. The belief on the part of the city officials was that the merchants had been forced to take out a license to avoid violation of Internal Revenue laws. The police believed that the men were not operating "blind tigers" (establishments in which liquor could be purchased without seeing the seller) but were instead "bona fide merchants" who had sold a concoction known as "Checkers," which had been analyzed by the federal government agents and found to contain 60 percent alcohol. The newspaper reported that the police had been waging "war on this beverage" and had almost completely stopped "the sale of the stuff…an alleged medicinal drink." The manufacturer had stopped marketing Checkers because of problems with the federal government. Therefore, the requirement that the Danville merchants who had sold the concoction pay for licenses was not an indication that the police were neglecting their duty. Rather, Mayor Wooding asserted that the licenses "had been practically forced upon merchants who had no intention of breaking the laws of the state."[97]

The grand jury empanelled for the most recent term of the Corporation Court had issued a number of indictments against the operators of blind tigers in an effort to break up the illegal liquor trade in the city. The *Register* noted that the witnesses included "many citizens who were known to be drinking men": "A result of the investigation was that indictments were brought in, and of all the indictments, only one of the parties, a Chinaman, was convicted in the Mayor's Court."[98]

The other nine defendants were acquitted because the principal witnesses against them had skipped town. Those witnesses who were present, including one who was taken out of jail (where he was serving time on an extortion charge), were called upon and examined by the mayor. They would make no direct statement "to the effect that they had either purchased intoxicants or seen others buy from any of those arraigned."[99] This matter of indictments brought and witnesses who refused to testify or left town before the trial was commonplace in the war between the temperance forces and the liquor law violators. In February 1905, the *Register* reported "another scene in the farcical political investigation of the blind tigers." This scene "was enacted in the Mayor's Court" when "two alleged liquor vendors of Craghead Street were arraigned."[100]

According to the *Register*, the witnesses in this case, although present, were of questionable character. In fact, "many spectators at the trail" realized that "the whole affair" had been "prearranged…to convict the accused." A prosecution witness admitted that she, a white woman, had been given fifty cents by Officers Hutson and Wynn to purchase whiskey from the alleged Craghead vendors.[101]

The other witness was a young white boy who had been "convicted in the Mayor's Court on a number of occasions for violations of the law." However, seized physical evidence was produced, and one of the defendants was convicted and fined $70 and costs with a thirty-day sentence in jail. His attorney noted an appeal, and the convicted man was released on a $100 bond. As for the second defendant, his case was dismissed because, according to the *Register*, "[t]he evidence against Pritchett was very weak, the witnesses for the Commonwealth, although apparently attempting to tell the same tale, differed widely at times in their statements." A third witness, a crippled black man who was suspected of being engaged in the liquor trade, had been called to testify. In spite of his testimony, that he had bought some whiskey from the accused man, and in spite of the testimony from the two police officers that "a drunken crowd loitered around Pritchett's place…and that they had seized a gallon of whiskey found in Pritchett's stand," the case was "promptly dismissed."[102]

What these two cases demonstrate is that liquor charges were not always successfully prosecuted. What they also highlight is the kind of proactive policing that officers in Danville engaged in with regard to liquor law violations. Investigations were undertaken. Suspected blind tigers were kept under surveillance and often raided. In February, a series of raids of tigers took place. On February 19, the *Register* reported that three blacks were in jail awaiting trial on the charge of selling liquor without a license.[103] On February 21, the newspaper reported that the cases against four blacks had been dismissed in Mayor's Court because the evidence was conflicting and not enough to convict. The procedure for building solid cases against blind tigers was obviously less than perfect.

During this time, there was some suspicion of corruption on the part of Danville police officers with regard to illegal liquor operations in the city.

The mayor appeared before the Ordinance Committee of the city council to request permission to employ detectives to investigate the illegal liquor business in the city and the rumors of police involvement. Two private detectives from the Baldwin Detective Agency arrived in town, worked on the case from February 1 to February 18, 1905, and reported back to the mayor and city council that liquor could be bought in the city by "giving money to parties." The names of these parties were given to the chief of police and to the March term of the Corporation Court grand jury. The detectives also informed the city council that the amount of illegally sold liquor in the city was greatly exaggerated. Moreover, they could find no grounds for suspecting that any police officer was derelict in his duty.

It should be noted that there were certain farcical elements to this investigation by the Baldwin detectives. Mr. Lee Ligon, the owner of a poolroom where the detectives had made their headquarters, claimed that the detectives might have been induced to "doctor" the report and that the secret investigation was not the best-kept secret in town—the detectives had gotten intoxicated and told people in the poolroom about their mission. Because of this charge, the council appointed a committee to consider whether or not they should pay the $262 Baldwin Agency bill. The committee concluded that the detectives had executed their duties adequately, and in subsequent testimony by the detectives before the grand jury, Mr. W.B. Baines, the proprietor of the Bell Restaurant, and his two black cooks were indicted. Mr. Baines was acquitted. The two blacks were convicted.[104]

Later that year, in September, a city council committee was formed to review the liquor ordinances and determine if they were sufficient. The committee recommended that new ordinances be enacted with regard to the now licensed saloons in the city. These new ordinances forbade screens or obstructions that would block the view of passersby into the saloons. The ordinances also forbade billiards or other games in saloons. A notable aspect of these ordinances was that the committee suggested that the saloons be required to obey written notices from parents, wives or guardians not to sell or give liquor to minor children, inebriate husbands or wards. The council adopted an ordinance forbidding persons to purchase or procure liquor for minor children. It also placed a $500 tax on liquor licenses.[105]

In October 1905, Mr. W.P. Hodnett, president of the city council, moved that a "Secret Service Committee" be appointed. The committee would consist of two members of common council and a member of the board of aldermen and be charged with employing a special detective whenever it was deemed necessary for "purpose of ascertaining and reporting any and all violations of the laws of our city." The committee would be completely independent of "all officers and citizens" and make quarterly reports to the council. The motion was referred to the Finance Committee to consider the $2,000 appropriation for a secret service fund.[106]

When Judge Aiken of Corporation Court heard applications for the sale of liquor in 1906, he issued seventeen saloon licenses and two for wholesale beer dealers. But, in 1907, the grand jury submitted a memo to Judge Aiken drawing his attention (and that of Mayor Wooding) to the fact that there was evidence that several saloons in the city were failing to comply with the city ordinance regarding screens and obstructions.[107] In January 1908, the Anti-Saloon League presented a petition to Judge Aiken for a special election. The wets and the drys ran campaign advertising side by side in the *Danville Register*. However, the drys succeeded in carrying the day, and Danville again voted out liquor.

During this period, the chief of police, R.E. Morris, appears to have been particularly vigorous in his efforts to enforce the laws against liquor offenders. In January 1908, Mayor Wooding fined Morris five dollars for conduct unbecoming a police officer because he used profane language toward a carpenter whose son had been arrested drunk and clubbed by one of Chief Morris's officers.[108] In February 1909, Chief Morris was reprimanded by Judge Aiken of Corporation Court because Morris had

Main Street looking west, Danville. *Photo by Alice Green.*

made an objectionable remark to a juror in a blind tiger case. The juror had been one of those who had acquitted a woman named Grace Bell. Chief Morris accosted Mr. Howard Salzman as he was leaving the courthouse and asked, "How much money or how much beer did you all get for turning Grace Bell aloose?"[109]

That same month, Morris was the subject of an investigation in Mayor's Court regarding the shooting of Nero Shaw, "a negro chicken thief." Morris had stopped Shaw on Main Street on Friday morning the week before to question him about the basket of chickens he had. Shaw tried to run, Morris grabbed his coat and Shaw bit Morris's hand. At that point, Morris shot Shaw in the leg when he refused to let go. Shaw tried to flee again, and more shots were fired. Since there were no witnesses, it was Shaw's word against that of the chief of police. Shaw claimed that he had been shot while he was running away. He was found guilty of stealing the chickens (five of which belonged to a woman who lived on Wilson Street) and fined five dollars with a sentence of sixty days in jail. As for Morris, Mayor Wooding acquitted him of wrongdoing but stated that there had been too much use of their firearms by police officers recently. He stated that a police officer "had no right to fire except in a felony case," not to frighten a fleeing suspect.[110]

Back in court again in 1911, Chief Morris was fined $10.00 and costs after an investigation by the mayor revealed that he had assaulted John C. Destine, "an aged resident of Stokeland and Confederate veteran, while the latter was under arrest Tuesday afternoon for drunkenness."[111] Morris had committed this particular assault on the street as he was taking the man to the station house, and a number of merchants had witnessed the incident. But Morris, his deputy sergeant and a police officer all claimed that the man had fallen out of a chair. Destine, the victim, had no memory of the incident, and the mayor fined him $2.50 for public drunkenness. To Chief Morris and his men, he stated that any member of the Danville police force who could not stand being cursed without committing an assault had better look for another job.[112]

This injunction by the mayor was unnecessary in the case of Chief Morris, because shortly thereafter, in March 1911, Morris was identified as a man named Thomas Edgar Stripling who was wanted for murder in Georgia.[113] Stripling had killed a man who he alleged had attempted to assault his sister and then had sworn to kill Stripling himself. Both Stripling and his brother-in-law were charged, even though it was Stripling who had shot the victim. Stripling escaped from prison and lingered near his home in Georgia for a time. He was finally persuaded to leave. After moving about and taking various jobs, he settled in Danville. At the time of his unmasking as Stripling, Morris was living with his wife and ten children, including two infant twins.[114] The *Register* noted that there was a lesson to be learned from the Morris-Stripling incident: that preference should be given to "home men of known and proven reliability."[115]

This matter of police behavior is relevant here because the police constituted an important interest group in Danville. During much of this period, the police department appears to have been split into factions. In 1908, Mayor Wooding had won the mayoral election by a "handsome majority" when he defeated Green Williams, a man who had been police chief in Danville in the 1890s. The wets in Danville considered the reelection of the mayor their victory. The *Register* estimated that Wooding had probably received 90 percent of the anti-prohibition vote.[116] That same year, the mayor was added to the six-member Police Commission. When the mayor had sworn in the new police officers earlier that year in March, he had observed that there was some friction among the officers, and he urged them to try to work together in harmony. He also added that he had been hearing reports that police officers were using profanity and cursing prisoners and that this must stop. Any officer found guilty of profanity would "be dealt with according to the law."[117] At the same time, the Police Commission had reelected Chief Morris, the abuser and profaner, for another term by a four-out-of-six majority.

Morris had defeated J.R. Bell, the police sergeant who had succeeded him as police chief when Morris was exposed as Stripling. Bell, who had been on the force for thirteen or fourteen years by 1911, was of "good old Virginia stock."[118] In 1922, Bell was still the chief of police, and the department was split into two distinct factions. Mayor Wooding and the two police commissioners he had appointed were supporters of Bell. An officer named Martin had the support of the three police commissioners appointed by Judge Withers of Corporation Court. When the Bell faction won, three officers who had supported Martin were dismissed.[119]

While these conflicts within the police department were taking place, it is reasonable to assume that there were also some divisions about law enforcement policy, particularly with regard to public order crimes such as liquor offenses. A month earlier, in January 1922, the Law and Order League had noted that there were "certain frictions and shortcomings" within the police department.[120] That same month, the members of the league discussed Mayor Wooding's ruling on the necessity of properly filled-out search warrants. The Anti-Saloon League was already expressing its concern about the lack of vigor the mayor was showing in enforcing the liquor laws by monitoring the sessions of Mayor's Court. The *Register* reported that on one such occasion in 1921, H.O. Kerns, president of the Anti-Saloon League, and W.T. Shelton, the state prohibition officer, were present in court and "bowed their head in approval" when the mayor was harsher than usual and imposed jail sentences on liquor law violators.[121]

In 1924, the Anti-Saloon League was still displeased with how liquor laws were being enforced in the city. It held a mass meeting to make an appeal for better law enforcement. Yet in April of that same year, Mr. Elliot, secretary of the police department, observed that there had been a "distinct reduction in the number of Mapp Act violations and the receipts by the Police and Sheriff's Club." The club received a $10 bounty on every offender convicted for violation of the state liquor law. At the same time that he reported this reduction in arrests, Mr. Elliot also reported that the club was in "good condition," with a balance of $1,500.[122] This money was used to secure a $500 life insurance policy for each officer, with the premiums on the thirty-four policies being paid by the treasury. So, obviously, the Danville police did have some incentive for enforcement of the liquor laws even if the antiliquor forces were not satisfied with the results of their efforts.

When C.K. Carter assumed the position of police justice, he began enforcing the laws from the bench in a manner more to the liking of the antiliquor interest groups. In 1925, the WCTU commended Carter on his "effective service."[123] By May 1926, the number of arrests for drunkenness was the lowest in twenty years.[124] Whether this was due to the deterrent effect of Carter's more strict enforcement policy or to the availability of alcohol to get drunk on is debatable. According to the *Register*, some offenders during this dry spell were substituting "canned heat," or denatured alcohol, for the real thing.[125] This meant not only that they continued to present a law enforcement problem, but that they were now a public health concern as well. At any rate, there was an increase in the number of liquor law violation cases appearing in Corporation Court after Carter became police justice. Looking at sample years between 1900 and 1930, more convicted offenders appealed from Carter's court in a six-year period than had from Mayor Wooding's court in twenty-four years.

PROFILE OF LIQUOR LAW OFFENSES

Much of the illegal liquor activity was centered in the downtown area on Craghead and Union Streets. Throughout the period, restaurants, groceries, pool halls, social clubs and, occasionally, hotels were places where illegal liquor sales flourished. However, blind tigers were also frequently operated in private homes. In February 1909, the *Register* reported: "The sensational crusade on the blind tiger industry in Danville is being continued and there are now twenty-one cases pending before Mayor's Court for illicit traffic in intoxicating beverages."[126] The newspaper noted that four more warrants had been issued and that a raid had occurred the day before on Main Street. The *Register* predicted that with large crowds expected to attend, the trials would "in all probability" be moved to the Corporation Court.[127]

Convictions in Mayor's Court could be appealed in Corporation Court. Of those individuals appearing in Corporation Court from 1900 to 1930 on appeals or on indictments from the grand jury, the majority were white (see Table 1).

TABLE 1: LIQUOR LAW VIOLATORS IN CORPORATION COURT

	Black	White	Total
Male	152	218	370
Female	42	17	59
TOTAL	**194**	**235**	**429**

These 429 liquor law cases represent approximately 24 percent of the 1,798 cases appearing in Corporation Court from 1900 to 1930. They account for 20 percent of the 972 cases involving black offenders and 28 percent of the 826 cases involving white offenders. For black females, the liquor law cases account for 37 percent of the total 112 cases, and for white females 34 percent of the total 50 cases. For black males, liquor law violations accounted for 18 percent of their 860 total appearances in Corporation Court, and for white males 28 percent of the total 776 cases.

When a defendant noted an appeal, a security bond was routinely required to ensure the defendant's appearance in the next term of Corporation Court. Some black offenders, even with the profits they may have been reaping from the liquor trade, might have been unable to provide the security bond or to find a bondsman who would provide it for them. Therefore, this group would not have been reflected in the sample. As noted earlier of these offenders, both black and white, some were repeat offenders.

A small group of eight offenders in this sample committed both public order crimes and more serious offenses. One such offender was Marshall Gilliam, a white man who accumulated fourteen charges against him between 1904 and 1912. Ten of the charges were for liquor law violations, one each for larceny and fornication and two related charges of felonious assault, one of which was dismissed and the other reduced and disposed of with a sentence of ninety days. In 1912, he was charged with fornication with a black female of ill repute. He was also charged with another liquor offense and placed on a $500 bond for good behavior (as he had been on at least three other occasions). At this point, he disappears from the Corporation Court records (at least for the sample years). It is possible that he was one of the whites who left town when the mayor initiated the "blockade" of the red-light district in 1914.

A black man named Lewis Robinson also had a long history of offending in the Danville community. Robinson was mentioned often in the pages of the *Danville Register*, where he was described as notorious in his ability to evade punishment. Between 1902 and 1922, he was charged with at least twelve offenses (fifteen if he was the "Louis" Robinson who appears in the records in 1924 and 1925). Robinson's offenses, although mainly liquor law violations, also included crimes such as keeping a disorderly house and running a gambling establishment. Like Marshall Gilliam, he appeared in both Mayor's Court and Corporation Court. He also has the distinction of having been pursued by the federal authorities for his liquor activities. But throughout the sample years, there is no record that he ever paid a fine of more than $100 or served more than six months in jail. The most costly bond he was ever assessed was $1,000 for his future good behavior. This amount was reduced to $500 in an appeal in Corporation Court.

What Robinson, Gilliam and the other offenders in this group of eight illustrate is the pattern followed by some liquor law violators in committing other, related public order offenses, such as keeping disorderly or gambling houses. Another interesting fact about this group is that these offenders seem to have often been associated with a lawbreaker of the opposite sex. Four of the eight, including Robinson, had a spouse who had also been charged with public order crimes. Robinson's wife, Sarah "Jack" Robinson, was in court in January 28, 1905, on a liquor charge. She had been convicted in a recent term of Corporation Court of illegal sale of whiskey. She was being arraigned for operating a blind tiger on Craghead Street, "over Long Well's old place." She was convicted and fined fifty dollars and costs for the city, twenty dollars and costs for the state. She was sentenced to thirty days in jail. The warrant sworn out against her by the police had been based on information provided by Mr. M.C. Whitman, who owned a hostelry on Main Street. He admitted that he had voted for the prohibition ticket in the last election but also insisted that he sometimes went to the blind tiger to treat himself to a drink.

Robinson's defense attorney claimed that Whitman had tried to induce other men to buy whiskey from Sarah and her husband to secure evidence against them. In fact, Mr. J.E. Williams testified that Whitman had accosted him on Craghead Street and offered him $0.50 to go buy whiskey from Robinson. But Robinson had declined to sell it to him. Whitman was fined $2.50 for contempt of court when he called Williams a liar, but the fine was remitted when he apologized. Two police officers testified that the house on Craghead Street was on their beat and that they had noticed "numbers of people going in and out" and become suspicious. Chief of Police Akers was called to testify about the "reputation" of the place. Mayor Wooding reserved his decision for ten days and placed Robinson on bond of $100.00 to ensure her appearance in court the following week.[128]

The white male offender, Marshall Gilliam, was associated with a black madam named Lucy Fields. She accumulated three other charges during the sample years, and as did Gilliam, she disappeared from the court records in 1912.

DISPOSITION OF LIQUOR LAW OFFENDERS

Overall, based on the available data, the fines and sentences given both blacks and whites seem to have fallen within a set range. The sentence and/or fine given an offender seem to have been determined, at least to some degree, by the offender's prior record. Having read the reported proceedings of Mayor's and Police Courts and studied the records of individual offenders, it seems that there was no significant difference in the disposition of black offenders in relation to whites. However, what (on the face of it) appears to be equity in terms of fines may not have been because black offenders as a group may have had fewer resources with which to pay the fine or the bond that they were assessed and therefore would have been more likely to end up serving time in jail.

Overall, of the 194 black offenders who appeared in Corporation Court from 1900 to 1930, 96 (49 percent) were sentenced to confinement (on average for about two months); 79 (34 percent) of the 235 whites who appeared were jailed (on an average for about three months, with more extremes of sentence within this group). During this period, the range of fines for both blacks and whites was from $5 to $250 dollars. In 1909, $5 was the most common fine for both blacks and whites. In 1915, 1921, 1924, 1927 and 1930, $50 was the most common fine for both races upon being assessed in Corporation Court.

COCAINE AND BLACKS

There was one type of law violation that police officers in Danville and elsewhere in the South attributed mainly to blacks. The white South feared cocaine use by blacks, believing that blacks who use the drug "might become oblivious of their prescribed bounds and attack white society."[129] During the Prohibition era, poor southerners and particularly blacks "were alleged to turn to cola drinks laced with cocaine or to cocaine itself for excitement as a result of liquor scarcity."[130] Although there was no evidence that cocaine contributed to "crime waves" among blacks, it was "the anticipation of black rebellion which inspired white alarm." The fear of the cocainized black coincided with the peak of lynchings, legal segregation and voting laws all designed to remove political and social power from blacks.[131]

Among the most incredible beliefs about cocaine was that it made blacks invulnerable to ordinary bullets and gave them super strength.[132] There is no solid evidence for widespread use of cocaine by blacks in the South. However, cocaine was available without a physician's prescription, "and the 'lower classes,' particularly in 'dry' states, found they could get a jolt which took the place of hard liquor. Bars began putting a pinch of cocaine in a shot of whiskey."[133] By 1900, state laws and ordinances were being enacted with reference to cocaine. In 1902, Virginia reported to a committee of the American Pharmaceutical Association, which was investigating the acquisition of the drug habit, that there was "an enormous growth in the cocaine habit among Negroes."[134]

In 1908, the *Register* reported that cocaine use and sale had become a problem among Danville blacks. According to the newspaper, only a few years prior not much of the drug had been used or sold in the city, but then an "influx of roustabouts and other desperate negro characters from the coal fields of West Virginia and other public works south of this city" brought in an element who used the drug and taught local blacks to use it. In 1908, a situation allegedly existed in which many of the blacks being arrested had a package "of the stuff" on their persons. The *Register* noted that in Danville, as in other cities in the state, the drug was being used by the "worse element" of the black population. The *Register* asserted that "most of the wild, unlawful acts of a good number of the colored men in the city" could be attributed to the fact that they used cocaine. But because it was sold "so quietly," it was almost impossible for the police to do anything about the problem.[135]

A month later, the *Register* expressed more general concern about drug use and abuse. In an editorial titled "The Cocaine Habit," the newspaper asserted that victims were "filling jails, insane asylums, and almshouses." The police were having little success in enforcing the law, and druggists were involved in distribution. Historians have found that early twentieth-century laws regarding drug use were enacted at least in part because white native-born Americans perceived the "dangerous class" (made up of new waves of European immigrants and nonwhites) as a threat. In Danville, blacks who sold or used cocaine were seen as deviants who threatened the moral and social boundaries of the white community. The police waged a continuous effort to repress the crime, but as in liquor law enforcement, they hit snags.

In 1910, for example, eight blacks were indicted by the grand jury of the Corporation Court for selling cocaine. They were acquitted by Judge Aiken because the police had failed to have the suspected drug analyzed. The *Register* observed that although the police knew that the habit was "flagrant among Negroes of lower and criminal types," they had a difficult time ascertaining exactly where the purchases were being made. The police believed that most of the cocaine in the city was distributed by blacks from distant places and resold by peddlers.[136]

There is no record of any drug case appearing in Corporation Court during the sample years. Thus, all of the available data about the occurrence of this offense in Danville comes from the *Register*'s reports of cases involving cocaine, and it is impossible to reach any conclusion about the sentences meted out to drug offenders.

GAMBLING

In 1902, a number of informations were filed in Corporation Court against gambling houses in Danville. In 1906, there was an ordinance on the book that prohibited gambling in the city. A person who kept or maintained an apartment, house or room where games of cards or chance were "habitually played for money" could be fined not less than five dollars nor more than fifty dollars and serve not more than thirty days in jail. The police often raided such houses. For example, in 1908, a gambling house operated by Lewis Robinson was raided, and eight or ten white men were found playing cards for money. As mentioned above, Robinson had a long police record. For this offense, he was fined fifty dollars and given four months in jail.

Gambling was one of those public order crimes that produced a fairly stable population of offenders. It was a commonplace offense during the early twentieth century. The biographer of a Danville police detective reports that during those years dice games and card games were continuously being raided, particularly on Friday and Saturday nights:

> *At the nip joints, which were plentiful, games went on from time to time in a small way. From these small games there developed the greater number of disturbances, due to the fact that there was not much concentration on the game, and also because of the whiskey element…Someone would get cut from a wild slash of the knife, and a police investigation would follow. In the games of this character there were so many reasons for a fight that it was just as inevitable as sunrise.*[137]

Clearly, there was a law enforcement rationale for breaking up these games. However, gambling and the accompanying disturbances presented an order-maintenance problem for the police rather than a clear threat to racial or social boundaries. Of course, it might be argued that the fact that white men patronized gambling houses run by black proprietors such as Lewis Robinson violated racial mores. But this kind of race mixing was not the equivalent of whites and blacks sitting together during public events at Hampton Institute (a black college in Virginia). It was instead the kind of backdoor association that had always gone on between some blacks and some whites in the South and that was as much a tradition of the informal structure of race relations as "racial purity" was of the formal. Moreover, the games, except for the penny ante games that were played in alleys and on street corners, occurred out of the respectable public's eye. It was, therefore, sufficient in terms of boundary maintenance that the gambling ordinance was on the book.

In Mayor's Court, the fine paid by gamblers climbed from what seems to have been a standard $2.50 in 1909 to fines that ranged from $16.95 to $25.00 in 1921. Then in 1923, the amount charged fell again, so that in the thirty-two cases collected in a Mayor's Court sample, fines range from $5.00 to $11.00. There is not enough data available to reach any conclusions about possible disparity in the fines given blacks as compared to whites. Raids by police officers seem to have been aimed at both races.

From 1902 to 1924, twenty-one cases of keeping a gambling house appeared in Corporation Court. There were repeat offenders in this category, such as Charles Gee, a white man who was charged with this offense four times during the period of 1902–8. Wyllie Williamson, who was black, had three such offenses lodged against him between 1904 and 1915. There were others such as Lewis Robinson, primarily a liquor offender, who had a sideline in illegal gambling as a gaming house proprietor.

Again, it is difficult to say if there was any significant difference in the sentences or fines given blacks as compared to white offenders. A snapshot of two years, 1909 and 1912, shows that three offenders, all black, received jail sentences of thirty days each. All of those found guilty during these two years were fined. The fines for black gambling house operators during the period ranged from twenty dollars to fifty-five dollars. For whites, the range was five dollars to twenty-five dollars. As a group, these offenders tended, as did liquor law offenders, to make cyclical appearance before the court to be fined, jailed and/or placed on bond. Of course, as pointed out earlier, there were other occasions when the police simply failed to make their case against such offenders.

PROSTITUTION

Like drinking, gambling and the sale and use of drugs, prostitution flourished in the red-light district of the city. Sometimes the local press provided a glimpse into the lives of the women who lived there. In July 1906, Reverend William Magbee, superintendent of the Children's Home Society of the State of Virginia, came to Danville to find two children who were believed to live with Maude Young and Susie Fox, "women of ill fame" in the red-light district. Judge Aiken and Mayor Wooding granted Magbee a decree to take the children. But they were gone.[138] A few months later, in October, a black physician, Dr. A.L. Winslow, was called to attend when Nettie Fox, Susie's sister, killed herself by taking carbolic acid. According to the *Register*, several hours had passed while efforts were being made to "secure" a physician. An hour after Dr. Winslow reported to the scene, Dr. W.O. Lee arrived to take charge. It is not clear why it was difficult to get a doctor to come to the house. The woman had lived over an empty storehouse on Craghead Street, a location that the newspaper described as being in the Tenderloin.[139] In another case, in February 1908, the *Register* reported that Bessie Gray, a "laudanum fiend," had been turned from her home in the red-light district.[140]

In October 1913, twenty women whose characters were questioned by the police were summoned before the mayor to give accounts of themselves. This action was taken when law enforcement officials became aware that women were arriving in twos and threes in the area that had formerly been Danville's red-light district. This area had been broken up and closed down by grand jury action earlier that spring, but it seemed that two white men had arrived from Richmond and were preparing to open houses of "ill fame." The police believed that it was an effort to "re-open the segregated district." Therefore, the women who might be involved in the undertaking were called into Mayor's Court for an inquiry concerning their "past records and future aspirations."[141]

The success of Danville officials in eradicating the red-light district in the downtown area is indicated by an action of the Virginia Board of Charities and Corrections. At the 1915 annual meeting, the board commended Mayor Ainslee of Richmond and Mayor Harry Wooding of Danville for their efforts in eliminating vice areas in their respective cities and for their interest in civic betterment.[142] However, four years later, women of suspected ill repute were still a part of the local landscape.[143]

In 1919, the *Register* titled an editorial "A Local Problem Calmly Reviewed." In the editorial, the newspaper pointed out that the young women being detained in the local jail because they were infected with venereal disease were entitled to due process. The *Register* noted that although its "entire sympathy was with the ends sought by the current campaign," it could not approve the course of the government agents. According to the newspaper, the young women lodged at the jail were being subjected to the diet, environment and meager comforts of such custody when they had not been adjudged criminals or even accused of any crime. Although the nation was still nominally at war, the *Register* asserted, the country was not under martial law, and the rights of its citizens could not be suspended.[144]

The city council was making some effort to deal with the problem. That year, the Committee on Health reported that a number of the women who had been arrested and placed in jail had been acquitted by Mayor Wooding, but while they were being detained, it was discovered upon examination by a physician that eight of the women had venereal disease. These women were turned over to the United States Public Health Service physician for "treatment and disposal." The difficulty was that there was no local facility for their quarantine and treatment, and the council had appropriated no funds for sending them away to be treated at the government farm in Warwick County, Virginia. The Committee on Health recommended that temporary facilities be set up in the city jail and placed at the disposal of the health department for the quarantine and treatment of cases until more convenient quarters could be arranged. It advised establishing a city farm for the detention, care and treatment of such women.[145]

However, there are occasional items in the *Register* throughout the period recounting episodes in which women of "low character" or named prostitutes were involved in activities such as indecent bathing, fighting, robbery or other offenses. In episodes during the 1920s and 1930s, farmers in town to sell their tobacco and find entertainment sometimes fell prey to a "disreputable woman" and woke up in a hotel room the next morning with their wallets missing.[146] There are also newspaper reports of other instances in which social agencies intervened to remove children from the care of their prostitute mothers. There are no data for the lower courts or for Corporation Court on the dispositions and sentences given women charged with prostitution. In one Mayor's Court case in 1918, a white prostitute was fined $24.95.

Vagrancy

During this era, vagrancy laws were enacted and used to control perceived troublemakers, particularly young men who were mobile and blacks who were not engaged in what whites perceived as useful employment. In Danville, an indigent black population was of concern to whites for a number of reasons. One of these reasons was that in the winter, when the tobacco factories were not at work, some blacks, particularly women, applied to the police, who administered the relief program for "winter assistance." The January 1905 *Register* observed that these women were a strain on the system. Making matters worse, they seemed to have an aversion to the employment they might have had "working in the homes of white people."

These women, however, were not wandering vagrants. They were a part of the resident black population. Of more concern were black males, particularly those who came from outside the city. In 1909, the *Register* quoted, with approval, a comment by Booker T. Washington, African American educator and race leader, to the effect that if white people in the South "will close their kitchen doors to the shiftless negroes, nine-tenths of the race friction that occurs will be eliminated because these negroes will have to go to work." The newspaper agreed and suggested that in Danville such men were being fed at kitchen doors by black cooks. These men, the *Register* asserted, would continue to "pick up a precarious living by their wits and petty crimes" as long as they were "fed by the women of the race." The paper continued: "The congregation of this idle negro criminal class around barrooms, pool rooms, snack houses and gambling joints emboldens the individual and teaches him lessons in crime."[147]

In the spring of 1909, the commonwealth attorney, Thomas Hamlin, and the police force inaugurated a crusade against vagrants. During the course of this crusade, seven young white men were arraigned in Corporation

Court on the charge of being of bad fame and character and having no visible means of support. They were required to furnish bonds for their future good behavior.[148] In October of that year, the newspaper reported a day when twenty more young white men were summoned to Mayor's Court on vagrancy charges. After they had posted bonds, several of these men either found work or left the city.[149]

In Danville, the vagrancy ordinance was enforced against both idle blacks and unattached, rootless young white men because both represented a threat to the stability of the community and were a repudiation of the dominant society values of home, family and hard work. However, it is arguable that because of the depth of white southern paranoia concerning blacks, the vagrancy statute would have been enforced more severely against blacks than against whites. But it is also possible that during the war years, 1917–19, the ordinance may have been applied with equal severity to "slackers" of either race. In December 1917, the city attorney informed the city council that there were already sufficient laws and ordinances to give the chief of police the "authority to close up pool rooms and such other places where persons without visible means of support congregate."[150]

As with prostitution, there is little data about the actual fines or sentences given vagrants. In 1907, three alleged vagrants (two black, one white) who appeared in Mayor's Court were assessed $2.50 each by Mayor Wooding. Under a related "loafing" ordinance passed in 1913, the idle could be fined "not less than $1 nor more than $10.00."[151]

SUMMARY

The fluidity of the interactions that occurred around vice crime and efforts to enforce these laws is captured in an episode that the *Register* reported in 1914. A police raiding posse composed of seven police officers had gone to Belleview Hill on a Sunday morning to raid "a notorious blind tiger." A "general melee" between the raiding party and a group of black men left six injured. A man named Harris was taken into custody after a "pitched battle with over a hundred Negroes." Later, the officers ran "the gauntlet of a crowd of white men who were bent on taking away from the officers their prisoner" before they could get him to the city jail. As a result of this second encounter, the six white men who tried to stop the automobile were taken into custody, too, "after a lively scramble." City Health Officer C.C. Hudson was kept busy for an hour "sewing up scalp wounds" and other injuries. The officers "came out unscathed save for a few scratches," but their clothes were "half-torn" from their bodies. It is not clear at this point why the six white men tried to take Harris from the police, whether they were vigilantes who wanted to take justice into their own hands or allies who were involved in some fashion with Harris's operation. What does emerge from the account is the sometimes raucous quality of these encounters.

When the case reached Mayor's Court, Commonwealth Attorney John W. Carter swore out a warrant against Police Officer Harris, charging him with the felonious assault of Art Gibson, who claimed that the officer had knocked him unconscious without provocation. Mayor Wooding set a bail of $15 for the six white men and set a $250 security bond for the black man, Harris. The security bond for Harris was set at the request of Police Justice Fits, before whom the cases would come to trial. To add another interesting twist to the proceedings, Attorney Harry Wooding Jr. was the lawyer representing the men.

The *Register* reported that the clue to the blind tiger's operation was that "half drunken negroes" could be found thereabouts on Sunday. The county police had gotten accustomed to dealing with the "many affrays." After keeping the place under surveillance, Harris was identified as the suspected operator of the blind tiger. The six white men were supposed to have an interest in the operation. Half drunk, they had wanted to take both the prisoner and the confiscated beer. But the police had not used their guns during the operations. They had used blackjacks and the butt ends of their pistols to knock three or four of the black men cold before the rest of the men retreated.[152]

In 1934, after national prohibition had been repealed, the Citizens' League for Promotion of Temperance and Law Observance in the City of Danville ran an ad urging a vote for state control of liquor sales to prevent an "uncontrollable, unlawful, and vicious bootlegging system" from continuing in the city.[153] However, photographs that can be found on the website of the Danville Police Department show that bootlegging continued to be a law enforcement problem well into the 1950s.[154]

CHAPTER 4

Rituals, Trouble and Repressive Justice

America's participation in World War I was a traumatic event in the life of the nation, and afterward nothing was quite the same. America had entered a new age. During the war, an atmosphere of hysteria existed concerning seditionists and foreigners. In the aftermath of the war, intolerance and bigotry grew and flourished. The country was plagued by postwar inflation, labor strikes and mail bombs directed to government officials. Some Americans feared a Bolshevik uprising. In Centralia, Washington, in 1919, members of the newly formed American Legion attacked the headquarters of the socialist Industrial Workers of the World (IWW). Throughout the country, the Ku Klux Klan and other vigilante groups engaged in propaganda campaigns and experienced surges in membership. With the spread of "extralegal justice," lynchings increased from thirty-four in 1917 to sixty in 1918 to more than seventy in 1919.[155]

Beginning in the summer of 1919, the country experienced an outbreak of race riots in cities as disparate as Longview, Texas; Chicago; Knoxville; Omaha; and Elaine, Arkansas. There were a number of reasons for this increased racial tension and the resulting violence. Uneasy whites feared the changed attitudes and military skills of black soldiers who had gone overseas during the war. Blacks streaming into northern cities to settle in congested areas would incur the resentment and hatred of unskilled white workers (many of them immigrants). At the same time, blacks and their leaders were demanding higher wages for their work, freedom from violence and an opportunity to participate in politics.[156]

LYNCH LAW

In the South, blacks who threatened the values, property and/or lives of the dominant white community were considered troublemakers of the first rank. Social, economic and physical boundaries separated blacks and whites. Most blacks and most whites observed these boundaries. However, those blacks who challenged the social or political status quo or who were alleged to have committed a crime might be perceived by white citizens as suitable candidates for extralegal justice (i.e., "taking the law into their own hands").

Historians have found that lynchings in the South were a public ritual—a ritual in which the rank and file of the community (ordinary citizens) participated. A lynching was the most drastic group response to a boundary threat by an enemy deviant. Between 1900 and 1918, about 190 whites and 1,312 blacks were lynched in the United States.[157] Between 1900 and 1930, about 2,054 people of both races were lynched in the nation, the majority of them black.[158] In the post–World War I era, federal anti-lynching legislation was first introduced in 1918 and failed to pass. In 1922, the bill supported by the NAACP and sponsored by L.C. Dyer, a white Republican from Missouri, would have made lynching a federal crime. The Dyer Bill passed the U.S. House of Representatives by a two-to-one margin. It died in the Senate by filibuster. Even so, the threat of federal intervention, a new awareness on the part of whites due to the NAACP publicity campaign and the migration of blacks out of the South (with resulting concerns about loss of labor) all contributed to a decline in lynching. Another factor in this decline was the disintegration of the Ku Klux Klan.[159]

In Danville, during the period of 1900–1930, there were two lynching episodes. Because this was the most extreme form of repressive justice the community could display toward a deviant or suspected deviant, those two episodes will be examined here. The first occurred in 1904. On July 15, a white Southern Railway flagman named James Armes was shot and killed in the railroad yard. There was a "vigorous search," and Roy Seals, a black man, was arrested. He was identified by a white man named Talbolt, who had been with Armes when he was shot. According to the *Richmond Planet*, the evidence was not conclusive, and many people, both white and black, were not convinced of Seals's guilt. Unfortunately, the Danville militia unit, the Danville Light Infantry, was in St. Louis, and lynch fever began to spread.

A mob of about seventy-five men, mainly railroad employees with handkerchiefs over their faces, gathered in front of the jail. But the police had been forewarned by the wife of one of the would-be lynchers who had gone to Mayor Wooding with the plot. They succeeded in standing off the mob by firing warning shots. A man named Daniel Talley, the mob leader and some other participants were taken into custody. Judge Aiken convened the grand jury at once (with E.G. Moseley among the jury members).

On Saturday, July 26, the cases against the principal participants in the lynching attempt were heard. Talley and three other men were fined fifty dollars each and sentenced to sixty days in jail. Appeals were noted. Three days earlier, on July 23, another participant had been given the same sentence, and a sixteen-year-old boy had been given thirty days in jail. The indictments against five other men were dismissed. The court reprimanded two members of the fire department whose headquarters faced the alley leading to the jail. These two men were cautioned for "using improper language toward the police force calculated to discourage them in the discharge of their duties and to inflame the mob." The grand jury commended the police force for the way in which it had dealt with the situation and handled the mob without bloodshed.[160]

According to the *Planet*, there had been general "consternation among the ranks of the lynchers" at the turn of events. Some left town; others went into hiding.[161] In February 1905, the *Danville Register* reported that a young white man named Elisha Williams had returned to town and been arrested. He was charged with being one of the participants "in the recent riotous demonstrations in the city" when an attempt was made to take the black prisoner Roy Seals from the city jail and lynch him for murder. According to the Danville newspaper, Williams had been one of the men indicted by the special grand jury. The others were "later fined and imprisoned," but Williams had left town and could only be taken into custody upon his return. At his arraignment in Mayor's Court, "a number of the witnesses testified that he was not on this side of the river when the attempt at lynching occurred." The *Register* predicted that although a further investigation was being made, the charges against Williams would probably be dismissed.[162] Williams's arrest came almost six months after the lynching attempt in front of the city jail.

In July 1904, the *Richmond Planet* had reported that "the majesty of the law" had been upheld in Danville when the would-be lynchers of Roy Seals were indicted by the grand jury and swiftly punished by Mayor Wooding and the court. A few days later, the *Planet* carried an editorial commending Mayor Wooding, Judge Aiken and Commonwealth Attorney Thomas Hamlin for their actions. By then it was known that Roy Seals was not the killer. A white man was the murderer and was "anxious to have the Negro convicted and hanged." The *Planet* extolled: "[T]he good white folks are not quite dead yet, and we see now that there are quite a number of them residing in the neighborhood of Danville, Virginia."[163]

The *Planet* gave Mayor Wooding consistently high marks as being one of the good white folks in Danville. As it noted on another occasion, the mayor "had declined to compromise in any manner a decision that he believes to be in accordance with his obligation and the principles of eternal justice." Thereby, he had proven himself to be "one of the finest type of Southern gentlemen."[164]

However, during the second lynching episode in Danville, neither the mayor nor the other good white folks in the community were able to prevent the fatal outcome. This 1917 episode has been referred to in regard to the black undertaker who was attacked by an angry mob. The *Planet* headlined its coverage of this story "Trouble in Danville, Virginia." The trouble was met with vigilante justice: "After killing a policeman and wounding six others, Walter Clark, a colored ne'er-do-well…was shot to death by armed citizens early this afternoon as he was driven out from his refuge in the rear of Wilson Street by flames started for that purpose."[165]

The episode had begun when a police sergeant named W.H. McCray and another officer named Riley went to arrest Clark. Clark was wanted for shooting, Fannie Betts Jennings, his common-law wife. Refusing to be taken into custody, Clark shot and killed McCray. Other officers rushed to the scene. For two hours, Clark held the police force at bay while "thousands gathered" at various vantage points, including rooftops, as word spread through the city. As the gunfire continued, six other men, three of them police officers, were wounded. When the house was set on fire by members of the crowd, Clark appeared in the doorway. He was met with a hail of bullets. He fell to the ground with his hair and clothes still burning. A mob dragged the body into the street, where the fire department put out the flames. The mob members then attacked the black undertaker who, they thought, intended to try to rescue the dead man's remains.[166]

By nightfall, the city was quiet. The *Planet* observed that although Walter Clark from all reports had not been "worth his salt," he had been keen-witted enough to "demand that Officer McCray show his warrant." No report released showed that the officer had one. The *Planet* concluded that Clark "crazed as he must have been by contraband liquor or insane emotions" had decided that his life was to be sacrificed and had "proceed to pay as dearly as possible." Although the *Planet* believed that Mayor Wooding and the police force had done their best to prevent a further loss of life, it asserted that the episode would never have happened if the police had allowed black citizens to capture Clark, because they would have been able to get him out "with little injury to themselves or anyone else." However, the black newspaper was pleased that "race feeling" had not prevailed: "It could not, for the causes and effects show that everybody there except Clark and the lynchers were in favor of upholding the majesty of the law."[167]

The NAACP reported, in its chronological list of persons lynched, that Walter Clark was lynched in Danville, Pittsylvania County. The "cause" was murder.[168] However, the *Danville Register* objected to any attempt to characterize what had happened as a "lynching." Responding to the coverage by other regional newspapers,[169] the *Register* argued that Clark had been crazed and dangerous, and although the men who had responded to the scene with guns had not been deputized as a posse, they had been there to assist the police. The *Register* pointed out that city officials, including the mayor and the commonwealth attorney, were at the scene and in charge. The house was set on fire after other attempts to get Clark out had failed. Even so, in its own first coverage of the event, the *Register* had described the crowd that had gathered as a "mob."[170]

Over a decade earlier, the *Danville Register* had addressed the matter of lynching. A column in 1906 referred to an atrocity committed in North Carolina by "Negro fiends"; in the adjoining column, the newspaper commented that if the North Carolina white men charged with the lynching of another black offender were freed, it would be "an encouragement toward lynching." Two days later, referring to these same lynchers, the newspaper noted that it was a pity that men who were "guilty of the disgraceful, cowardly crime of lynching are so hard to bring to justice." As the newspaper noted, although "we may dislike the idea of bringing them to trial in the U.S. Courts," that might be the only way that their punishment would be secured.[171]

As mentioned above, the threat of federal intervention was one of the forces that eventually served to curb lynch law in the South. But, as the *Planet* suggested, there were from the beginning forces in Danville that opposed this form of extralegal justice. Some white Danvillians who opposed lynching may have been concerned with morality and justice. Others may have been equally concerned with the reputation of the community and the avoidance of trouble that would disrupt the even flow of life in Danville. For members of the white commercial-civic elite, the departure of blacks from the city because of the racial climate would have been detrimental to their pocketbooks. Particularly in the tobacco factories, blacks provided a cheap labor pool.[172] These whites along with black members of the commercial-civic elite engaged in "conflict management" during racial episodes.[173] This was arguably an important reason why lynchings and lynching attempts did not occur more frequently in the city. However, Danville is also located in an upper South state, and Virginia as a whole was less prone to lynchings than lower South states such as Mississippi, Georgia and Florida.

RACIAL CONFLICTS AND NEAR RIOTS

Lynchings in Danville may have been rare events, but clashes between blacks and whites were more commonplace. Fights, rock throwing and brawls were all reported in the newspaper. Shots were occasionally fired. In a 1915 editorial, the *Register* asserted that violence in Danville "must be curbed." According to the newspaper, there were "more cases of assault and fights in proportion to our population than almost any city we know." The *Register* was not referring solely to black-white violence. It was referring to a general problem. The reason for the problem, according to the newspaper, was a lack of training in "self-control" and a "proper conception" of the rights of others.[174] Whatever the cause, the resulting clashes were a law enforcement matter that brought both whites and blacks into court.

One such racial episode occurred in 1917, a few months before the lynching of Walter Clark. White soldiers and several black men had "what threatened to be a serious clash." The trouble began when a black man "in a restaurant was overheard by privates in Company N to make an obscene remark about white women and to use abusive epithet regarding soldiers."[175] The soldiers dragged the offending black man and two of his friends outside and tried to dump them into the Dan River. The police arrived, and the soldiers, on orders from their noncommissioned officers, released the men. The black men were taken to jail.

Mayor Wooding had been called, but by the time he arrived at the scene, order had been restored and police officers were patrolling the area. Two of the black men were charged with having caused the disturbance. Grasty, the man who had made the remarks, paid the court clerk fifty dollars from a "wad of money." The other man who had been charged paid a ten-dollar fine. The charges against the third were dismissed.[176]

What is significant about this incident is that it shows black community leaders in the role of conflict managers. In an open letter to the *Register*, these members of the black commercial-civic elite performed a ritual of reconciliation. In the letter, they denounced the behavior of Grasty and his friends and pledged their own cooperation with the white community. The black leaders expressed their appreciation for "the prompt and efficient action of the mayor, commonwealth attorney and police force in quieting the disturbance that arose in our peaceful community." The leaders noted that this was a time when all passions should be "blended into one great natural spirit" of "patriotism."[177]

This was a strategic effort not only to restore peace in the city but also to acknowledge the boundaries of the dominant white community and thereby place themselves within them. In an editorial headline, the *Register* asserted that this was "A Time For Coolness and Self-Control." The newspaper characterized what had happened as the "offensive language of a mischievous young negro" that did not represent of the majority of black citizens. The newspaper stated that "only the best of cordial good feeling" existed between "representatives of the better elements of the two races."[178]

As for the *Richmond Planet*, it observed of the episode that "[t]he white toughs…were worse than the people they attempted to punish." The paper asserted that cooperation between the "the "better class of colored and the better class of white people" was necessary to "keep these elements under control."[179] At the same time, the black newspaper observed that black people would do well "to think more and talk less" and that the community of Danville should be careful not to allow a situation like "the massacre that occurred there many years ago" to happen again.[180] This last mention was obviously a reference to the Danville Riot of 1883. Undoubtedly, the black leaders in Danville also remembered "the massacre."

SERIOUS CRIME IN DANVILLE

Having considered lynch law and black-white racial violence, we should look at other felony offenses. The cases that were heard in Corporation Court from 1900 to 1930 provide an overview of how the criminal justice system in Danville responded to serious crimes.

Homicide

During the sample years, thirty homicide cases were tried in Corporation Court. In twenty-one cases (70 percent), the defendant was black. In nine cases (30 percent), there was a white defendant. Two of the white defendants were found guilty. Thirteen of the twenty-one blacks were found guilty of murder. According to the court records for two cases in which the death sentence was imposed, both involving black defendants, an appeal was in progress. There was no record of final disposition. The ten blacks sentenced to the state penitentiary were given terms ranging from one year to life in prison (ninety-nine years). One offender received a reduced charge and six months in jail. The sentence was available for only one of the white offenders found guilty. That defendant was given a term of three years in the penitentiary.

During the period of 1900–1906, at least nine men and two women in Danville died at the hands of other people. All of the accused offenders were male. In one case, the victim was a young man of unsound mind who was forced into the Dan River. In another episode, two black males allegedly beat a black male victim to death with sticks. On appeal, a new trial was granted in this case. In the Corporation Court records, only the victim's name is given. Additional information about the circumstances of the offense is sometimes obtainable in the instructions to the jury. The *Danville Register* is another source of information. Judging from the news items in the *Register*, such offenses, then as now, were often the end result of a quarrel between people who knew one another—whether they were friends, relatives or partners in crime.

In the sample years between 1909 and 1915, three men were allegedly killed by other men. A female victim was murdered by her husband. The only other case involved a woman who stood trial for allegedly leaving her newborn infant, sex unknown, in the stump of a tree.

In 1921, there were five homicides in Danville, the greatest number of any of the years sampled. That year, three of the defendants were black, and two were white. One case, in June 1921, caused a great deal of excitement in the community because it involved the death of Officer John P. Jones from a trap gun set by a black storeowner to discourage "storebreakers." The use of trap guns (or spring guns) to discourage burglars and "housebreakers" were occasionally reported in the media. However, in such cases, the court had generally held that setting a trap for burglars to protect one's home from intruders was different from setting a trap to protect an unoccupied property from thieves.

In the Danville case, Irvin Pierce, the black storeowner, was also a socialist. After a highly publicized trial with a well-known white defense attorney (and a change of venue), the charge was reduced to second-degree murder, and Pierce, the defendant, was sentenced to fifteen years in prison.[181]

Finally, aside from such high-profile cases, there were other cases in which the original charge of murder was reduced to involuntary manslaughter. Five such cases occurred in the sample years of 1900–1930. Three of the five were cases of involuntary manslaughter involving automobiles. One of these offenders was a white female. The vehicular homicides reflect something that Danville had in common with the rest of the nation. As more drivers took the road in cars, both they themselves and unwary pedestrians were at risk.

Rape

In the twenty-three rape cases appearing in Corporation Court during the sample years from 1900 to 1930, eighteen (78 percent) of the defendants were black. The other five (22 percent) were white.

It should be noted that rape trials were a relatively rare event in Danville during this period. In six of the sample years (1906, 1909, 1912, 1915, 1918 and 1924), no rape cases were prosecuted in Corporation Court. But in 1921 and 1930, there were seven rape cases each year. The race of the victim is not given in the records.

Worthy of note is that such cases sometimes involved child victims. Six cases between 1900 and 1906 involved victims under the age of seventeen. In fact, four of these victims were under the age of fourteen. One high-profile case in 1905 involved an alleged attempted "criminal assault" on a twelve-year-old girl by a local representative of the Standard Oil Company. The two families lived next door to each other, and there had been some conflict involving the behavior of the siblings of the alleged victim. In the preliminary hearing, Mayor Wooding expressed "his opinion that one of the other of the parties deliberately lied."[182]

In 1921, four defendants, tried separately, were charged with raping the same thirteen-year-old female. In this case, two of the men were each given five years in prison. One was found not guilty. The charge against the other was dismissed. In another case, the victim was over eighteen but "feebleminded."

That same year, 1921, a forty-two-year-old laborer was charged with the rape of four juvenile victims in a case sent up from Juvenile and Family Court. He was found not guilty of one charge, bills of not true were returned by the grand jury on two of the remaining charges and on the fourth charge he received a sentence of one year in prison. Another defendant, a thirty-six-year-old textile worker, was also sent up from Juvenile and Family Court in a case involving two victims (both with his last name). He was found not guilty.

In two cases tried in 1927, both victims were under the age of twelve. Each defendant was given eighteen years in prison.

Robbery

Overall, from 1900 to 1930, there were thirty-four robbery cases prosecuted in Corporation Court. About 82 percent (twenty-eight cases) involved a black defendant. White defendants were involved in the other 12 percent (six cases) in which race of defendant is known. It is impossible to determine from these data whether robbery was predominately an intraracial or interracial crime in Danville. But it was an offense in which there was at least minimal participation by female offenders. Two female defendants in this sample of Corporation Court cases robbed male victims. One was sentenced to a year in prison and the other to two years. Robbery was also a crime in which offenders often seemed to have partners in crime. In all but two cases occurring during the sample years, the victim of the offense was male.

Twenty of the twenty-eight black defendants were found guilty, receiving an average sentence of five and half years. Sentences ranged from one year to eight years. According to the records, no white defendant was sentenced on a robbery charge during the sample years.

In 1915, the *Danville Register* reported that extra policemen had been assigned to patrol Main Street in the "Banking block." This was the area from Wall Street down to the corner of Craghead Street. Chief of Police Bell had made this decision at the suggestion of "one of the directors of the Commercial Association." The patrol officers would be on duty from half past 12:00 p.m. to half past 2:00 p.m. when the bank employees were out to lunch. A "wave of bank robberies" that were "novel" and "exceeding daring" had been occurring across the country, including Richmond. The newspaper noted that the need to protect the banks in Danville showed that they were "no longer small town affairs."[183]

Aggravated Assault

For the years sampled, there were 174 cases of aggravated assault (felonious assault or malicious wounding) tried in Corporation Court. Of this group, 116 of the defendants were black and 58 were white. Eighty (about 69 percent) of the black defendants tried for aggravated assault were found guilty; 94 percent of this group went to jail or prison. By comparison, twenty-eight (48 percent) of the white defendants were found guilty; 53 percent of those found guilty were imprisoned.

Among the cases tried in Corporation Court during this period, four involved an alleged assault on a police officer. The offender and the outcome appear below (Table 2):

TABLE 2: AGGRAVATED ASSAULT OF POLICE OFFICER

Year	Officer	Defendant(s)	Disposition
1900	Collie	Gallispie	true bill (no final disposition given)
1904	Gee	Williams	4 years
1904	Gee	Ware	90 days
1904	Hall	Hicks	not true bill
		Dillard	10 years
		Carter	not true bill

The defendants in these four cases were black. Both Joe Williams, Officer Gee's assailant, and Ryland Hicks, who was alleged to have assaulted Officer Hall, had long police records. Williams's record included housebreaking, "carbreaking" and robbery. Between 1904 and 1906, Hicks was charged with six different offenses, including felonious assault, robbery, grand larceny and carrying a concealed weapon. In 1906, he was given eight years in the penitentiary for robbery. Jack Dillard, sentenced for the assault on Officer Hall (on the testimony of Ryland Hicks), was also a known felon.

Aside from the assaults on police officers, there were also cases involving victims and alleged offenders who shared the same name. These were probably cases of domestic violence. There were fifty-seven felonious assault cases in Corporation Court during the sample years 1909, 1912 and 1915. At least three cases appear to have involved relatives. There was one case involving both a burglary and a felonious assault. Twenty-three felonious assaults were tried in 1918 and 1921. Four involved a female as victim. In two cases, a female was the defendant. But, as was true in all the years sampled, the majority of the cases involved male defendants. Of the fifteen cases between 1924 and 1927, ten cases involved male victims and three involved female victims. Two assaults were committed by females, one on another female and one on a male victim.

Burglary

Burglary was not a crime that was tried frequently in Corporation Court. In all, twenty-two cases appear in the sampled years. In twenty (91 percent) of the cases, the defendant was black. White defendants (9 percent) account for the other two cases. In cases with black defendants, thirteen (65 percent) were found guilty. In one of the two cases, the white defendant was found guilty. This lone white offender received a sentence of two years in the penitentiary. For blacks, sentences ranged from ninety days to eighteen years. Between 1900 and 1906, at least one case involved a husband and wife as codefendants. He was found not guilty. She received a sentence of five years in the penitentiary.

The items stolen in eleven burglary cases between 1900 and 1906 ranged from a chicken worth thirty-five cents to clothing, jewelry and money. Four cases involved business owners as victims (commercial burglary). Two of these businesses were owned by well-known white members of the community, J.O. Boatwright and H.L. Ficklen. The number of burglaries tried in Corporation Court ranged from five, all involving houses, between 1909–1915 to three in 1918–21 and then three again in 1924–27. There were no burglary trials on record of 1930.

However, there was another type of offense that accounted for a number of the felony property offenses in Danville.

Housebreaking/Storebreaking

From 1900 to 1930, there were 204 cases of housebreaking or storebreaking (which appears to have included entry into storehouses that were adjacent to or attached to a dwelling or building) in Corporation Court. Blacks accounted for 152 (74 percent) of the defendants. Whites made up the other 52 (25 percent). About 124 (81 percent) of the 152 blacks tried in the court were found guilty, and 34 (65 percent) of the 52 white defendants were given a guilty verdict.

Between 1900 and 1906, there were 109 cases of housebreaking/storebreaking, 12 cases involved multiple offenders and 24 cases involved businesses. In 1909 and 1912, some businesses were victimized more than once. In all a total of twenty-five businesses or firms were broken into (out of an overall total of forty-two break-ins). One case involved a housebreaking in which the three black defendants were alleged to have stolen whiskey from a black woman suspected of operating a blind tiger.

In another case in 1909, two young white men were charged with breaking into a clothing store on Union Street. The two men, who had broken into the store on a Friday night, made off with two suits, two pistols and other articles. In a related case, a white woman, who lived on Craghead Street, and a man were charged with receiving stolen goods.[184]

In 1918–21, there were twenty break-ins during these two sample years. Six firms were entered. One was the target of three different defendants. In 1924–27, thirteen housebreakings or storebreakings occurred. Finally, in 1930, twenty break-ins occurred in this year. Seven firms were victims.

Carbreaking

Carbreaking was an offense involving breaking into and stealing from railroad cars. The principal target of this offense was Southern Railway. During the sample years, from 1900 to 1930, thirty-two cases of carbreaking were tried in Corporation Court. Twenty-one (66 percent) cases had black defendants. Eleven (34 percent) had white. Thirteen (62 percent) of the black defendants were found guilty. This was true of four (36 percent) of the white defendants. Sentences for blacks ranged from sixty days to five years. For whites, the range was from one year to three years.

In January 1905, the *Register* reported "Syrians at Fair Grounds Found Possession of Stolen Property." The police had raided a place that was "supposed to be the rendezvous of many thieves" who were making "depredations on the property of Southern Railway and various merchants about the city." The two Syrians, Castor and Cassie Ali, who may have been husband and wife, had a store in the vicinity of the fairground. They were arrested and charged with receiving stolen goods, including fifty pairs of shoes, two cases of tobacco and several boxes of assorted clothing. The newspaper noted that convicting the vendors of stolen property was "one of the greatest evils that the police have to deal with."[185]

Grand Larceny

Grand larceny accounted for 176 of the cases appearing in Corporation Court during the sample years. Black defendants were charged in 107 (61 percent) of the cases and whites in 69 (39 percent). Grand larceny is tied with aggravated assault as the felony offense category having the most (fourteen) black females as defendants. Six white females were charged with grand larceny, only one with aggravated assault. It is likely that the appearance of females as grand larceny and aggravated assault offenders is related to the participation by females in other criminal activities such as prostitution and illegal liquor. Prostitutes, for example, sometimes "rolled" their clients. For the sixty-two blacks found guilty of grand larceny, the range of sentences was from thirty days to eight years. For whites, sentences ranged from ninety days to six years.

Third Offense Petty Larceny

In Virginia during this period, third offense petty larceny was a felony. During the sample years, forty-seven (94 percent) blacks were tried for this offense. Three (6 percent) whites appeared in Corporation Court on this charge (although thirteen whites and fifteen blacks appealed petty larceny convictions). For blacks found guilty, sentences ranged from thirty days to five years. For whites found guilty, the average time served was twelve months.

SUMMARY

Blacks were overrepresented, relative to their less than 35 percent of the population, in every felony category considered. From the news items appearing in the *Register*, one receives the impression that black offenders did generally murder, rape, rob and assault other blacks rather than whites. However, there is also reference in 1921 during the alleged "black crime wave," and occasionally during other periods, to offenses committed by blacks on white victims. Blacks and whites were also sometimes involved in mutual assaults during fights and brawls. As for white-on-black crime, young white men and boys appear to have been the chief offenders in this category. Boys sometimes harassed blacks in public places (by, for example, throwing rocks or snatching a hat). Young white men engaged in the same practice of "having a little fun," sometimes going a step further and physically assaulting a black man or woman.

Again, though, it is difficult to say how much personal crime was interracial, whites were clearly sometimes involved on assaults on each other. For example, in 1909 a crowd gathered when a dry goods clerk and a farmer got into a fight that spilled onto Main Street. The trouble between the two was "of long-standing." They were separated before they could do serious damage to each other and fined by the mayor when they appeared in his court.[186] Another episode in 1921 made the front page of the *Register*.

A nineteen-year-old named Cousins had died from blood loss after being slashed with a knife that a father-in-law was wielding. Cousins's brother had tried to intervene. According to witnesses, the fight had been the "culmination of a quarrel" that had lasted more than twenty minutes and taken place at the corner of Union and High Streets. All three men were employees of the cotton mills and had "recently come to Danville from Charleston."[187]

Understandably, with regard to property crime, both black and white offenders seem to have preferred more affluent white rather than black targets for crimes such as housebreaking or storebreaking, although businesses owned by blacks were sometimes victimized by black offenders. In the cases of grand and petty larceny, black offenders seem to have chosen both black and white victims, while white offenders seem to have chosen white victims. From the data and from what we know historically about the impact of the "color line" on black life in the South during this era, there is good reason to suspect that the processing of blacks through the system and the length of sentences handed down was not without bias. As legal scholars have found, a "dual system" of justice evolved in the aftermath of the Civil War that reflected the social, political and economic inequities that were institutionalized in the segregated South.[188]

CHAPTER 5
Jails and Juveniles

In 1904, the Virginia General Assembly passed a law requiring every city with a population of ten thousand or more to have a council composed of two legislative bodies (board of aldermen and common council). In Danville, these councilmen were drawn from six wards, three councilmen each (according to council minutes). Until the push by the Good Government Club for a single-body council in 1924, the ward system prevailed in Danville. Unlike the ward system in cities in the Northeast, the system in Danville seems to have functioned without rampant corruption and to have provided working men and small merchants some opportunity to participate in city government.[189] An examination of two topics discussed during meetings and actions taken by the city council provides us with additional insight into the environment in which crime and justice occurred in Danville.

JAIL CONDITIONS

In 1904, the commissioners appointed to inspect the city jail reported to Judge A.W. Aiken of Hustings Court. The commissioners (J.F. Rison, W.P. Horner and R.W. Robinson) reported that the building was "sufficient for convenient accommodation of prisoners confined therein, and safe and well-secured and sufficiently heated."[190] The commissioners noted that the area of the jail reserved for male prisoners was thirty-five by forty-four feet and contained "four rooms, one dungeon and the water closets on the ground floor." There were five additional rooms on the upper floor. The space for women was only twenty-five by thirty feet, with four apartments for sleeping. The jailor in charge of the facility appeared to be performing his duty properly and "in accordance with law." The commissioners found no alcohol in the jail, and the food being provided to the prisoners seemed to be "wholesome and sufficient."

Among the primary recommendations from the commissioners was that new locks be installed on the sleeping rooms in the male section (because of concern about the old locks in the event of fire). In fact, the commissioners noted the need to repair the floor in the male section of the jail that had been damaged by an earlier fire. To save on fuel in the winter, the commissioners recommended that a door of sheet iron, glass or wood be placed on the outer door leading into the vestibule or water closets. They also recommended bunks rather than mattresses be used as bedding. As they noted, it would be an "economy" to the city in the long run to have bunks built into the wall. Finally, the commissioners reported there was a need to construct a vestibule or second door in the male section of the jail because in the past two jailors had been "injured when prisoners of desperate character rushed the open door." W.A. Cook had been killed, and Sam Womack had been knocked down and had his hip broken.[191]

In August of the next year, the *Register* reported that the chain gang officers had been instructed to shoot at escaping men. This new policy was in response to a number of escapes. Mr. R.M. Gee had appealed to the board of police commissioners to be given this authority. The hope was that the threat would be sufficient that the officers would not have to actually use their guns.[192]

The matter of prisoner escapes came up again in 1907 when jailor R.L. Woolfolk was censured because a prisoner named Albert Adkins and others had escaped on January 25. Woolfolk was said not to have taken proper care of the jail keys. He had left the keys with unauthorized persons in the office of the chief of police rather than locking them up. On the day of the escapes, Mr. John Hall had obtained the keys from the chief and then left a door unlocked. If Marshall Gilliam and Will Hughes, two of the prisoners, had not intervened, there would have been more escapes. The jailor was not present when the escapes occurred.[193]

In another matter, under an ordinance that year, the mayor could "by his warrant" direct the city jailor to order designated prisoners to be put to work on city streets and public works. Each prisoner would have a ball and chain, and the prisoner could not refuse to work.[194]

By 1908, the conditions at the jail had deteriorated. Conditions that had been sufficient four years earlier were now "deplorable." The jail commissioners, R.B. Graham, Green Williams and Dr. C.W. Pritchett, reported that the jailor had failed to discharge his duties. The list of derelictions included:

- Failure to whitewash the women's section twice a year.
- Trash and filth on the floors and windows.
- Insufficient bedding for the prisoners, many of whom occupied the same cot; there was no place for mattresses except on the floor.

However, the commissioners found the kitchen clean and the food "plentiful and wholesome." But both the women's and men's sections had problems with overcrowding. In the women's section, there were four cells (six by seven by seven) and as many as eighteen women incarcerated at a time. The men's section, according to jailor Vaughan, could house as many as sixty-eight prisoners. But there were only ten cells (nine by twelve by ten) and one dungeon. The commissioners recommended at least twelve cells in the women's section and at least twenty additional cells in the men's section. In addition, there was a problem with poor ventilation that needed to be remedied, as did the sanitary conditions. There were no provisions other than basins for face and hand washing in the women's department. The men's section had an iron tank for bathing but no way to heat water. The commissioners' recommendations included a dining hall and court for exercising on the first floor.[195]

Judge Aiken required the city council to make changes. The *Register* reported that by statute the judge of the court was the person who made the decision about "what improvements are necessary" and when the jail was "in proper condition." The judge planned to appoint a committee of citizens to investigate conditions at the jail and make recommendations.[196] Later that year, the city council appropriated $18,000 to improve the city jail based on the recommendations that it had received from the Committee on Public Buildings.[197]

In February 1909, eight steel cages arrived at the jail and were installed by an expert from the manufacturing plant in Salem.[198] By 1910, the *Register* reported that Danville had both a new jail and the "largest number of prisoners for many months." Fifty-four men (thirty-one black, twenty-three white) and four women (all black) were being held. The newspaper noted that most of them had committed petty offenses and, after appearing in Mayor's Court, been locked up when they were unable to pay their fines. Among the jail population were also several prisoners held over for the grand jury and several who had been sent from Martinsville. Twenty-five prisoners were working on the chain gang at the city rock quarry.[199] However, the city council requested the Committee on Public Building to investigate "what additional expenses" were now being borne by the city that had formerly been borne by the jailor.[200]

The Committee on Public Buildings reported to the council again in May 1911. This time the concern was the rumors that substandard materials had been used by Camden Iron Works when the jail cells were installed. The committee stated that escapees were the responsibility of the jail officers on duty. It had been "reliably informed" that prisoners had been allowed "a certain amount of freedom, and after dark, when they should have been in confinement, have been seen on the streets." Although the Camden Iron Works was not at fault, the company offered to make "certain changes" in the rods and other equipment of the first cells that had been installed to made them more secure. That could be done for under $300. W.K. Anderson, the subcommittee chair, recommended a "certified copy" of a section of the report be forwarded to the commonwealth attorney for whatever action was deemed necessary.[201] Presumably, this was the section of the report dealing with the neglect of duty by the jail officers.

In 1915, the council took two actions related to prisoners. In the Ordinance on Feeding Prisoners, it made the Committee on Streets and Bridges responsible for contracting for prisoners' food and clothing. It also gave chain gang guards police power.[202]

The *Danville Register* reported in 1917 that there was unrest among Danville police officers, who wanted more money and were receiving better job offers. In the same article, the newspaper reported that the jailor, a city sergeant, said that he had been operating the jail at "a personal loss" for nearly a year. There were only a small number of prisoners, and the cost of feeding them was increasing.[203]

By 1921, there were other problems at the jail. This time, jailor J.P. Brooks and Frank Cousins, the superintendent of the city farm, were reprimanded by the grand jury in Corporation Court. A prisoner named Charles Gray, convicted on a Mapp Act (liquor law) violation, had been given "excessive liberty." According to witnesses, Gray had been on the street and at his home and restaurant on Union Street. Both Brooks and Cousins were warned not to allow this to happen again, with Gray or any other prisoner. Brooks asked for, but was not given, the names of the witnesses who had testified against him. As for Cousins, he was ordered to see that Gray "engaged in manual labor like the other prisoners." The police were ordered to arrest Gray if he was found out again.[204]

An article in the *Register* in May 1922 had the headline "Jailer Brooker [*sic*] is Running Two Boarding Houses?" One of the houses referred to was a "soup house" in back of the courthouse where transients were accommodated until they were either given more permanent housing or discharged. However, there was another house on Wilson Street that the jailor was allegedly renting and where he had "already secured three women boarders." Seen entering and leaving the house "quite frequently," the jailor was, according to the newspaper, giving "this recent extension of his boarding house business his personal and careful supervision and attention." The matter had become public when one of the leaders of the Law and Order League was informed of the new boardinghouse. It was assumed that this leader was the person who had reported the matter to the police. However, the newspaper noted, it was not yet clear what action might be taken.[205]

In July 1922, the *Register* reported that a strike by chain gang prisoners had caused Judge D. Price Withers to discuss with the city council the need to change the rules and regulations governing the city jail and the chain gang. Under the new chain gang regulations:

- Unless given a medical excuse by the city health officer, city prisoners would serve on the chain gang for ten hours per day.
- A daily list of prisoners eligible for service would be posted by the jailor.
- The superintendent of the city farm would have custody of the gang and could do whatever he and the guards required to prevent escapes.
- If a prisoner refused to work, he could be whipped by the officer in charge (within reason). He could also be put on bread and water.
- All prisoners would be kept chained between the jail and the quarry.
- Chain gang guards could enter the jail to inspect prisoners.
- Jailors shall search prisoners entering the jail.
- There would be no gambling.
- Lights would be out at nine o'clock.

According to the *Register*, the reason for these new regulations was that at the time of the strike, Judge Withers had discovered there were "no hard set" rules in place. After being unable to obtain the rules used in the Richmond penitentiary, the city attorney had drawn up regulations based on those used by the army.[206]

Aside from concerns about regulating prisoners' behavior, the city also needed to provide for their medical needs. In March 1925, Judge Withers of Corporation Court appeared before the city council to make a request concerning the jail. He asked that the third story be provided with a concrete floor to allow the isolation of prisoners with infectious diseases. In June 1926, Dr. Hawkins, the physician who tended the prisoners, asked city council that the third floor of the jail be divided into rooms for the segregation of contagious cases and to "provide rooms for both sexes with certain sanitary improvements."[207] In 1934, the state health commission reported that the jail was maintaining a high standard. The medical service was satisfactory.[208]

JUVENILE JUSTICE

At the end of the nineteenth century, reformers began to create a juvenile justice system that would remove children from the adult criminal justice system. In Danville, in the early twentieth century, city officials, educators and reformers expressed concern about providing for the educational and recreational needs of juveniles and dealing with the special issues presented by juvenile delinquency. In January 1905, an advocate for reform of state juvenile laws stopped in Danville during a tour of nearly every state with his wife. From New York, Dr. Orne, had come to Danville by way of Richmond,

The James F. Ingram Justice Center, Danville. *Photo by Alice Green.*

and he planned to spend several weeks in Danville. He was trying to create "public sentiment" favoring a general curfew law and a juvenile court law. Orne was concerned about the "children of the streets" and the increase in "child crime." Having an interest in "the negro race," he planed to "preach to them while in the city."[209]

Nationwide, during this era of the "child savers," there was concern about the employment of children as laborers. In 1914, a photographer from the National Child Labor Committee was in Danville to catalogue the employment of children under the age of fourteen at various jobs, from lunch carriers and messengers to work inside the mills and factories.

In 1918, the city was still without a juvenile court. Two probation officers worked with delinquent children. During the three years before 1918, sixty boys and youths had been paroled by the court and placed under the supervisor of two probation officers, J.R. Tucker and E.A. Prescott.[210] In May 1922, Judge Ricks addressed the Public Welfare Committee of the city council. He asked that steps be taken to create a juvenile court that would be presided over by "a proper officer" and in which "young boys and girls might be properly tried and paroled under the supervision of a guardian appointed by the court." He asserted that this was the surest way to create good citizens rather than hardened criminals.[211]

In November 1922, the city council considered how to provide a clerk and a full-time probation officer to work with the judge of juvenile court. The chairman stated that the best solution seemed to be to pay the executive secretary of the Community Welfare Association, Miss Margaret Maxon, a flat salary in lieu of all other donations to the "Outside Poor." In December 1922, Miss Maxon became the clerk for juvenile court.[212] By 1923, Judge Harris was requesting $200 to buy furniture and supplies. A clerk was brought in from Richmond to install the record system for the court and instruct Miss Maxon, the Danville clerk, in her duties.[213]

During this era, one of the concerns of children's advocates was that juveniles have an opportunity for healthy recreation. In June 1926, a committee of the city council considered the matter of playground facilities for black children. Health officials had said that there was a "great need" for such facilities. Several black citizens addressed the council committee, offering to level the ground if property could be found for the playground. Mr. W.P. Boatwright said that he was pleased to see "so much interest being shown by the colored people in the development of their youth." He assured the petitioners that the committee was in favor of providing for the playground and would present the matter to the council.[214]

Efforts at prevention aside, the juvenile court was still busy eight years later, in 1934. For the year ending in June, the court reported having dealt with 321 white boys, 47 white girls, 232 colored boys and 61 colored girls. Of these children, some were defendants and some dependent or neglected children. The count of those described as being ungovernable or beyond parental control was 12 white boys, 15 white girls, 14 colored boys and 18 colored girls. Of those charged with an offense, 183 children were charged with stealing or attempting to steal. The juvenile court was also dealing with adults who had been charged with child abuse or cruel treatment: 88 white men, 6 white women, 152 colored men and 24 colored women. Other adults were charged with contributing to the delinquency of a minor: 26 white men, 6 white women, 18 colored men and 7 colored women.

Of course, it is difficult to know what these data mean with regard to parents or other adults and these children. As is true today, the perceptions of poor people and those of the middle class may have been different. Poverty may have directly affected the ability of adults to care for their children. But the numbers give us some sense of the type and volume of cases being processed.

CHAPTER 6

The Winds of Change

THE 1930 MILL STRIKE

As in other mill towns, Riverside Cotton Mills offered an extensive "welfare plan" for workers. The benefits provided by textile mills for their workers often included housing, medical care, schools, baseball leagues and libraries/reading rooms. These benefits helped to fill the gap for employees before a time when "large-scale government-sponsored and charitable welfare" was available.[215] But aside from any benevolent motives on the part of the southern mill owners, providing benefits helped the companies to deal with labor issues:

> [I]ndustrial leaders concerned with growing problems of absenteeism, worker turnover, and unrestrained labor unrest developed complex welfare plans to provide services to their employees in exchange for greater loyalty, less turnover, and consistent labor peace.[216]

Providing these benefits to workers allowed the corporations "to extend their control beyond the workplace and into the community.[217] They were able to exercise some influence over how the workers used their free time. Many services were provided on site, but use of community services might also be encouraged. For example, in January 1905, the *Register* reported that a chapter of the Young Women's Christian Association (YWCA) was being proposed by a board of "lady directors." Temporary space had been secured in Roberts' Memorial Hall on the Northside. The local YWCA would be open to all economic groups and would provide reading and writing rooms, hot and cold baths, a gymnasium, a boardinghouse register to help young women find lodging and educational clubs and Bible classes. The committee was soliciting donations from local businesses. The expectation was that the young women who worked in the factories and mills would be particularly interested in becoming members of the YWCA.[218]

In July 1919, H.R. Fitzgerald, the president of Riverside Cotton Mills, went beyond the usual types of benefits provided to workers. The *Christian Science Monitor* headlined an article "Cotton Mills Give Employees a Voice." The article explained that "through a 'house of representatives' and a 'senate,'" the five thousand workers at the Danville mills were being allowed to participate in governance. Fitzgerald had spearheaded an innovation that captured "national attention." This experiment in "industrial democracy" created a system in which the workers were allowed to participate in the running of the mills by proposing "legislation" to address their grievances.[219] Yet, over time it became clear that the workers' power to negotiate for major changes in the way the mills operated was still minimal. The workers had been allowed to address small issues but could not obtain higher salaries and better work conditions. They were particularly disillusioned by a company decision to cut their wages in late 1929. From the company's perspective, this was a rational response to a changed economic situation:

> *The postwar years had not been good one for the mill. Production and profits were down, and there were fears that the North Carolina textile strikes would spread northward. The mill had a reputation for fair wages and good employer-employee relations, but with the declining sales, management ended the economy dividend paid to employees and instituted a 10 percent wage cut.*[220]

For many of the workers, the best response to this action seemed to be to form a union. In fact, the idea of forming a union had been proposed thirty years earlier. In the 1890s, the American Federation of Labor (AFL) had tried to unionize southern textile workers. Because Danville's mills were "the largest in the South," they had seemed a "logical place to begin a unionization drive." The goal of the union was to improve working conditions by getting a shorter workweek. In the spring of 1900, employees at the Riverside Cotton Mills worked twelve-hour shifts six days a week, a seventy-two-hour week. The union was advocating for a ten-hour day. The company cut the length of the shift to ten hours in winter but retained the twelve-hour day in summer. The workers wanted ten hours year round and decided to join the AFL.

On March 30, 1900, Samuel A. Gompers, the president of the AFL, came to Danville to negotiate with company officials. When negotiations failed, the workers went out on strike. The strike failed, as the strikers found themselves facing "hunger and eviction" from company housing. Unlike the later strike in 1930, city officials, including Mayor Wooding, and leading merchants provided support to the union. Clergymen also organized to support the workers. This early effort at unionization occurred at a moment when there was some tension between the city of Danville and the Riverside Cotton Mills over matters such as the pollution of the city's water supply by the mills.[221] During the next two decades, these issues were resolved, and the attitude toward the mills became "one of civic pride and admiration."[222]

In 1930, the United Textile Workers of America (UTW) was attempting to organize in the South. The Riverside Cotton Mills, one of the largest and most profitable textile operations in the region, became a test case for unionization. Local 1685 was formed when seven hundred of the one thousand workers attending a rally with Francis J. Gorman, the first vice-president of UTW, paid the one dollar in initial dues and joined the union. Union officials then tried to negotiate with Fitzgerald for higher pay and better hours for the workers.[223]

The workers were challenging the company as the country moved into the Great Depression. But compared to some other states, Virginia was in a better position economically. Some citizens of Virginia already knew how to cope with poverty. Virginia combined "a diversified economy and conservative fiscal policies with a widespread poverty that was little influenced by economic fluctuations"[224] In 1930, two-thirds of Virginia's population lived on farms or in small towns. Even before the Depression began, "[l]arge segments of the population, especially blacks, mill workers, and subsistence farmers, lived in impoverished conditions."[225]

The 10 percent wage cut instituted by Riverside Cotton Mills moved the millworkers backward economically. Understandably, they wanted the money returned to their paychecks. In April, the union "put its case before the public."[226] Union members paraded from their headquarters on Loyal Street and up Main Street to Ballou Park. Their placards bore messages such as "We Are the Undesirables," "55 Hours Work for $13.50. Could You Live on That?" and "Discharged Because We Joined the Union."[227]

On September 29, 1930, the millworkers began the strike. The company sought an injunction from the Pittsylvania County Circuit Court to prohibit the strikers from picketing outside the mill gates at Southside or trespassing

The 1930 strike at Dan River Mills. *Courtesy Clara Fountain and Schoolfield Preservation Society.*

on mill property. An injunction was also sought and granted from the Danville Corporation Court.[228]

Over the next months, the dispute between workers and management "generated a considerable amount of violence and bitterness, especially as some strikers were evicted from their company owned homes."[229] These evictions were the "get tough" strategy adopted by Fitzgerald after his attempt to use persuasion had failed. His first strategy had been to have "loyal" workers try to convince others that the "outside agitators" were causing the problem. When this effort failed to dissuade the workers, he began to fire and evict the leaders of the movement. The excuse given for this action was not that they had joined a union but rather that their work was unsatisfactory.[230]

In early October, the *New York Times* reported that H.R. Fitzgerald had rejected an offer by Governor Pollard of Virginia to appoint a mediation committee. Fitzgerald in his reply to the governor said that there was "absolutely nothing to mediate" because there was "no real grievance." He said that if there had been grievances, the employers could have handled the matter "through their own committee any time."[231] Although the strike was notable in the beginning for the peaceful nature of the protests, by winter the tone of the strike had changed. The money and food provided by the union was running out. Some workers (called "scabs" by union members) were crossing the picket lines to take jobs in the mills. Incidents of strike-related violence increased (escalating from rock-throwing and name-calling to slashed tires and the bombing of an empty church in Schoolfield Village). The deciding event occurred when strikers blocked the road leading from Danville to the mills. Workers reporting for their shifts were turned back. Fitzgerald, the president of the mills, had his car physically lifted and turned back in the direction of Danville. These escalating clashes brought action by the governor:

> *When riots finally broke out on 26 November after forty mill workers had been jailed for unlawful assembly, the governor had to respond to requests from authorities in Pittsylvania County to send in the National Guard to end the turmoil.*[232]

After the militia had arrived, the *New York Times* reported "Danville Holiday Is Quiet." The troops on patrol in Schoolfield Village enjoyed Christmas dinner supplied by the Commissary Department at the mills. The strikers received a Christmas gift in the form of $500 from the Church Emergency Committee in New York. This infusion of funds was not enough to keep the strikers going. By January 1931, the strikers were out of food and money. Many of them began drifting back to the mill seeking employment. Fitzgerald rehired "loyal" employees, even some of those who were union members. Gorman declared that this was a victory of sorts. Fitzgerald denied it, saying that he had not recognized the union. Union leaders were not rehired:

> *The strike, which some say "was one of the most serious in Virginia history," ended on 29 January 1931 without the union either recovering wages or gaining collective bargaining for the workers. The strikers had been assailed by strikebreakers, evicted, and starved out, as Roxie Prescott Dobson* [a strike leader] *stated it, all for "nothing, just nothing."*[233]

Within one month, Fitzgerald was dead of a heart attack. On the day of his funeral, the looms in the mills went silent, and flags in the city were at half-staff. The millworkers joined the rest of the city in mourning Fitzgerald's death. His physician attributed his demise to the stress of the labor strike.[234]

THE GREAT DEPRESSION AND WORLD WAR II

When the strike was over, the mills did not rebound economically. The earnings of the mill were off in 1930 ("a disastrous year"), 1931 and 1932. Even earlier, in 1928, the *New York Times* had reported that the Riverside and Dan River Mills, "one of the largest textile plants in the South, had curtailed its operations." Because of "the stagnant condition of the cotton goods market," about 5,500 workers were being laid off. The mills' earnings rebounded in 1934, with "sales figures exceeding those of 1929."[235] But trouble was lurking for the industry as a whole. In 1935, the Textile Fabric Association appealed to President Roosevelt and Congress for protection from foreign competition.[236]

The tobacco industry also experienced a downturn. However, the tobacco interest was "considered nearly 'depression proof.'" Even though sales of factory-made cigarettes were down, "roll your own" sales were up. The dollar value of tobacco production in Virginia remained high, dropping by only 3 percent and recovering quickly.[237] There was a lag time before the industry began to feel the pinch of the Depression.

One of the creative responses by the industry to an economy that was badly battered and getting worse was the "tobacco queen." Danville sponsored the

Hylton Hall, Dan River Mills, Schoolfield, now closed. *Photo by Alice Green.*

first tobacco queen contest in 1934, and other cities followed suit. This was the equivalent of the "bathing-beauty revue" made wholesome by "invoking and altering rituals of rural life that had been familiar to white southerners for decades."[238] As prices for bright-leaf tobacco fell, sponsors of the tobacco queen contests in Danville and elsewhere "hoped to use beautiful women to stimulate business."[239]

But those at the bottom of the economic rung—blacks employed as tobacco workers—suffered. Already bound to seasonal work, they had their hours cut and found little to do after the season was over. Across the state, unemployed white workers "enjoying the preferences of white employers, dropped down to take jobs normally reserved for blacks."[240]

America's entry into World War II stimulated the economy on the homefront and provided new job opportunities for both blacks and women. During the war, the Danville mills boomed as they turned to filling military contracts. But during the war, certain types of crime apparently also increased. In 1943, Police Chief Watson announced that the police department was "widening the scope" of its drive against immoral behavior.

View of the Danville Dairy Products building and the surrounding commercial buildings, including the Ideal Bakery, circa 1946. *Courtesy Library of Virginia.*

93

Exterior view of Danville Knitting Mills and cars parked around it, circa 1946. *Courtesy Library of Virginia.*

Street scene of business district in Danville, circa 1946. *Courtesy Library of Virginia.*

The vice squad was ready to crack down "on certain hotels and other houses in an effort to end the rise in unlawful associations." The police had secured the cooperation of some of the hotels and hoped to have increasing success in "the campaign against immorality."[241]

In the aftermath of the war, a younger generation of businessmen replaced the prewar incumbents on the city council. This would pave the way for the annexation of Schoolfield Village by the city of Danville.[242] In 1946, the Riverside and Dan River Cotton Mills became Dan River Mills, Inc. By the 1950s, the textile industry and Dan River Mills were enjoying good times. In the *New York Times*, ads featured the company's slogan: "Dan River Runs Deep." The clothing in the ads was made from the mills' patented fabrics.

In September 1950, the Textile Workers Union asked to meet with management "to discuss the possibility of a wage increase."[243] Dan River was reported to fear losses because of wage negotiations with the CIO Textile Union. The corporate officers told shareholders that the union demand would add $12 million to operating costs. B.D. Browder, the vice-president

Interior view of a large Danville textile machinery, with a bolt of fabric fed through, circa 1940s. *Courtesy Library of Virginia.*

of Dan River Mills, blamed the union demands on northern union leaders who were injecting themselves into the situation.[244]

However, the textile workers at Dan River Mills eventually joined the strike that affected "41,000 cotton and rayon workers in six states." In April 1951, Dan River Mills and Spring Cotton Mills in Lancaster, South Carolina, had announced a 2 percent wage increase. The Textile Workers Union was not satisfied with the offer and charged that the mills were making excuses using federal wage regulations that, the mills claimed, restricted the amount of the raise they could offer.[245] Four days later, the union offered to end the twenty-one-day strike on Dan River Mills by submitting to arbitration. The company declined the offer. Among the strikers were military veterans. About 380, "dressed in uniforms or parts of uniforms, paraded in front of the main Dan River plant" at Schoolfield.[246]

By the end of April, the *New York Times* was reporting "Gun Battles Mark Cotton Mills' Strikes." The gun battle had occurred at the Royal Cotton Mills in Wake Forest, North Carolina. In Danville, there had been "numerous dynamitings in recent days, three men were arrested, and charged with the illegal possession of dynamite." One of the men arrested, John Howard Crew, was the business agent of the local union. Police said that they had found sticks of dynamite, percussion caps and fuses in his home.[247]

The strike began to wind down in May 1951 when the national union officials recommended ending the strike with federal meditation. Because of Dan River Mills' importance as an industry leader that set traditional wages, the mills "played a crucial role in the walkout." The local union in Danville survived the failed strike but lost much of its power because in its aftermath the company refused to deduct union dues automatically from the workers' salaries.

CIVIL RIGHTS

In 1946, Charles K. Coleman, a grocer and teacher, became the "first black to run for public office since the riot of 1883." He was defeated, but his candidacy "represented the aspirations of a new generation of blacks in the city." The Danville Voters League, an African American organization, set about registering black veterans and other blacks to vote.[248]

In 1954, the United States Supreme Court struck down the 1896 decision in the *Plessy v. Ferguson* that had established "separate but equal" as the rule of the land and legalized Jim Crow laws in the South. In *Brown v. the Board of Education*, the Supreme Court ordered the integration of all public accommodations (from water fountains to schools and amusement parks) "with all deliberate speed." In Virginia, as in other states in the South, this federal mandate was met with resistance.

In 1960, in Greensboro, North Carolina, a stone's throw from Danville, black college students staged sit-ins at the lunch counter in Woolworth's, and a new era of direct, nonviolent action was born. In Danville, students attempted to integrate the Danville Public Library, which was located in the Sutherlin Mansion (the "Last Capitol of the Confederacy"). The library was closed rather than have it admit black patrons. When it was reopened, the city had adopted a strategy of "vertical integration."[249] All of the seating had been removed from the library. Blacks could now borrow books but had to take them and go.

Among the black leadership in Danville, as elsewhere, there was ongoing debate about the tactics that should be used to overcome white resistance to integration. The local NAACP chapter, led by Reverend Doyle Thomas, favored the strategy that the national organization had followed with great success: the use of the legal system and the courts. The Danville Christian Progressive Association (DCPA), affiliated with the Southern Christian Leadership Conference (SCLC), favored direct action. The leaders who favored such direct action included Reverend Lendell Chase, Reverend

J.M. Langston High School, Danville. *Photo by Alice Green.*

Lawrence Campbell, Reverend A.L. Dunlap, Julius Adams and Arthur Pinchback. Adopting the SCLC model advocated by Reverend Martin Luther King Jr., they planned to stage sit-ins and demonstrations. They sought the help of the national SCLC. The Student Nonviolent Coordinating Committee (SNCC) also provided field workers.[250]

The demonstrations began on May 31. One June 5 and 6, protestors marched on City Hall and demonstrated at the Municipal Building. Judge Archibald M. Aiken, Jr., issued a temporary injunction that would later become permanent that limited the scope of protest.[251] Employing what can best be described as an innovative legal strategy, the judge convened a special grand jury and charged the protestors with violating the 1859 "John Brown law" by "conspiring to incite the colored population of the State to acts of violence and war against the white population."[252] This was the law that had been used in 1860 when John Brown, the white abolitionist, was convicted and hanged after leading the raid on Harpers Ferry, during which he had hoped to inspire blacks to rebellion.

Led by Mayor Julian Stinson, city officials moved quickly to adopt a strategy that would become a model for municipal resistance. The city sought and received injunctions that forbade mass protests. A newly enacted city ordinance specified that "demonstrators must be at least 18 years old, must picket in groups of six or fewer, only during business hours, and must march single-file at least 10 feet apart." The penalties for violation of this ordinance were "a $500 fine and up to 12 months in jail."[253]

The stance on the part of city government was that the trouble in Danville was the result of "outside agitators." Actually, there was some discussion among black leadership about the promises made by SCLC to support the Danville movement and the organization's failure to always follow through. However, it was also clear that the agitation for change was coming from Danville residents. The movement was seeking city jobs for blacks and desegregation of public facilities, including schools and hospitals.

During the summer of 1963, a series of arrests occurred. In court, defense attorneys objected to the antagonism toward the demonstrators that they felt Judge Aiken displayed.[254] They sought a change of venue and hearing by other judges. They sought to have the cases that Judge Aiken was sending to other cities moved back to Danville.

The civil rights groups continued to disagree about strategy, but the NAACP, led by Reverend Doyle Thomas, helped to provide lawyers and raise money to post bails. This was necessary because any resistance to the injunction forbidding demonstrations was considered grounds for

Civil rights demonstrations, Danville, 1963. *Courtesy Library of Virginia.*

Historic marker of the Bloody Monday demonstration in front of the James F. Ingram Justice Center. *Photo by Alice Green.*

arrests. The tension between the police and the demonstrators culminated on what is now known as "Bloody Monday." On this day, June 10, 1963, demonstrations occurred in the morning and again that evening. The police, commanded by Chief Eugene G. McCain, turned fire hoses on the demonstrators and beat them with clubs. Sixty people were arrested, and at least forty-seven were injured.

SNCC prepared a bulletin containing photos from the demonstration and the "Official Record of Hospitalized Demonstrators." The listed injuries of one of the demonstrators included "lacerations of head, fractured wrist, possible injury to back." Most of the other injured demonstrators had lacerations of the scalp and abrasions on arms and legs.[255]

The June demonstrations continued as "tension and apprehension was heightened by the murder of a Mississippi Negro leader."[256] The leader, Medgar Evers, was assassinated on June 12, 1963, as demonstrations were occurring in Danville and Cambridge, Maryland. What was going on in Danville had attracted the attention of the Kennedy administration. William H. Geoghegan, assistant deputy attorney general, was sent to Danville as the personal representative of Attorney General Robert Kennedy "to look into the Danville situation."[257] Geoghegan attempted to get the two sides—represented by the mayor's all-white Racial Advisory Committee and the black DCPA—to the table to negotiate.[258]

On June 21, the mayor met with twenty-three white restaurant owners to discuss "removing racial barriers." Motel and hotel owners were planning to meet later that week.[259] Even so, on June 23, the police went to High Street Baptist Church and arrested three members of SNCC (from outside the city). Meanwhile, two ministers—Reverend L.W. Chase, the pastor of High Street, and Reverend Hildreth W. McGhee—were on $5,000 bond after having been indicted for "inciting the Negro population to riot."[260]

On July 12, Martin Luther King Jr. came to Danville. The demonstrations had been going on for six weeks, and Dr. King, president of the SCLC, called on blacks in Danville to "fill the jails for freedom." He held a three-hour rally that evening that was attended by 1,200 people.[261]

As the protests were going on in Danville, on July 18 Reverend Campbell and about 100 demonstrators picketed outside the Dan River Mills offices in New York City. Protestors carried signs with messages such as "Dan River Mills Call Off Dogs Stop Police Bullies." Reverend Campbell told the press that Dan River Mills could "integrate Danville tomorrow" if it wanted. He pointed out the company employed 9,800 workers in Danville and "more or less" controlled the city because of its economic, political and social position.[262]

By July 31, Avon Rollins, a member of SNCC, was warning that if the demands of the protestors were not met, there would be "blood flowing in the streets." Accusations had surfaced about violent and brutal actions by city officials and police officers (such as pushing a young girl down some stairs and beating a crippled boy). Ironically, recalling the Danville Circular of 1883, some of these accusations appeared in circular published in New York by the Committee for Danville, Virginia.[263]

By August, the federal courts had halted prosecutions while they reviewed the appeals by the defense attorneys for the protestors who had been arrested. The chief judge urged the antagonists to use the time before the hearings to try to communicate with one another and find some solutions.[264] But on August 14, Charles Womack, a member of the Danville City Council, offered a resolution that the council appoint a biracial committee "to investigate possible infiltration of Danville Negroes by subversive elements."[265]

Later that month, the massive "March on Washington" took place, bringing 200,000 to the nation's capital. In Danville in the weeks that followed, the city officials would gradually back away from their earlier tactics. In late September, Judge Archibald Aiken rescinded his order requiring that 125 black defendants be tried in courts outside the city.[266] On October 17, 1963, Police Chief Eugene McCain announced that Danville would hire its first black police officer—the first since the 1880s. McCain said the applicant, William Wesley Terry, formerly a Houston supermarket employee, was the first black to apply (since 1951) who had met the requirements for the job.[267] However, overall the Danville movement had not achieved all that the leaders had hoped, having been "worn down and frustrated" by the tactics used by city officials.[268]

Largely excluded from good jobs in the textile industry until federal legislation gave them leverage, blacks began to bring lawsuits. These lawsuits allowed them to enter the mills "in large numbers, filling production positions that had previously been occupied by whites only."[269] However, even after they were hired, the "first wave" of African Americans in the mills "endured a great deal of discrimination." Their "main grievance was that they were restricted to lower-paying jobs."[270]

During this era, "virtually every large southern textile company was involved in class action racial discrimination suits. Among the major companies sued were Cannon Mills, Fieldcrest Mills, Cone Mills, J.P. Stevens and Company, and Dan River Mills"[271] In *Adams et al. v. Dan River Mills*, depositions were taken from black women who had "tried unsuccessfully to get hired at the Dan River plant in Greenville, Alabama."[272] Black men were also a part of this lawsuit. The lead plaintiff was Julious Adams, who had been one of the leaders of the civil rights protest in 1963:

> *Adams, a dyehouse laborer who emerged as a leader of a large group of black workers determined to improve their status at Dan River, had also been at the forefront of various efforts to end segregation in Danville. He was the treasurer of the local chapter of the Southern Christian Leadership Conference and was the lead plaintiff in the desegregation suit filed against the local school system. Adams helped enlist workers for the Dan Rivers Mills case and made the initial contact with EEOC.*[273]

SUMMARY

The changes that occurred in Danville between 1930 and 1963 reflected the groundswell of social change that began as the United States responded to the Great Depression and two world wars. Challenges to the status quo on the part of labor and blacks forced Danville to move beyond the concept of a community based on old divisions of race and class.

In 1959, Danville hired its first city manager, Ed Temple. The council-city manager form of government replaced the older council-mayor form.[274] This was a change from the days of Mayor Wooding, who had held his position of mayor long enough to earn a place in *Ripley's Believe It or Not!*[275] From 1980 to 1984, Charles Harris served as the "first black mayor of Danville." Before becoming mayor, he had been a city councilman for twenty years.[276]

Danville Past, Present and Future

Out on U.S. 58, a marker indicates the spot where on Sunday, September 27, 1903, the fast mail train on the Southern Railway route between Washington, D.C., and Atlanta plunged seventy-five feet from Stillhouse Trestle into the ravine below. Eleven people died. Thousands gathered at the scene. The disaster was immortalized as the "Wreck of the 'Old 97.'" In 1924, the ballad of the engineer who took the curve too fast as he tried to make up time was released, and in the next three years the recording sold over 1 million copies.[277] It was the first million-selling county music song—and the subject of a lawsuit about the authorship of the song. Modern audiences outside the South might have had their first exposure when bluegrass musicians Lester Flatt and Earl Scruggs performed the song on the television situation comedy *The Beverly Hillbillies*.

Another ballad, "The Night They Drove Old Dixie Down," more plaintive in tone, recalls the end of the Civil War and the Southern defeat from the perspective of a soldier. Written by a Canadian, the song was released on an album in 1969 by country-rock musicians The Band. In the song, "Virgil Cane…served on the Danville train," the Richmond and Danville train that was the main supply line to Petersburg and Lee's Army of Northern Virginia. Joan Baez's 1971 version of the ballad rose to number three on the *Billboard* charts.

In popular culture, the train between Richmond and Danville also played an important role in the mystery of the missing Confederate treasury. According to legend, when Confederate president Jefferson Davis and his staff fled Richmond, $500,000 (more or less) in currency, jewelry, gold coins and Mexican silver dollars was placed aboard a train to Danville. When the

Historic marker of the Wreck of the Old 97, Danville. *Photo by Alice Green.*

Freight train stopped at crossing, 2010, Danville. *Photo by Alice Green.*

Former downtown parking lot, Spring Street, Danville. *Photo by Alice Green.*

Closed and demolished Dan River Mills facilities, Schoolfield. *Photo by Alice Green.*

train left Danville, a portion of that treasury is supposed to have been left behind, probably buried in Green Hill Cemetery, which is owned by the city. Officials have refused to give treasure hunters permission to disturb the graves. However, in December 2010, an episode of *Brad Meltzer's Decoded* on the History Channel examined the alleged clues to the mystery of the "Confederate Gold."[278]

In Danville popular culture, there is also the story of two Danville girls—one married Charles Dana Gibson, the illustrator who created the "Gibson girl," the iconic image of the "New Woman" of the late nineteenth and early twentieth centuries. One of Gibson's models was Evelyn Nesbit, the Floradora Girl who married an unstable and jealous millionaire (Harry Thaw) who killed a famous architect (Stanford White) over Evelyn. Irene Langhorne Gibson, wife of illustrator Charles, was not directly involved in the 1906 murder trial in New York City that became the "crime of the century." But she and her sister, Nancy—who became Viscountess Astor and the first woman to serve as a member of British Parliament in the House of Commons—made up the fabulous Langhorne sisters. Their family had been wealthy before the Civil War, and they were the inspiration for the Gibson girls created by Charles Dana Gibson. In 1922, Nancy (Lady Astor) came to Danville and received the key to the city.[279]

Home of the Institute for Advanced Learning & Research, Danville. *Photo by Alice Green.*

Sign for the Institute for Advance Learning & Research, Danville. *Photo by Alice Green.*

Bridge and geese at Riverwalk Trail, Danville. *Photo by Alice Green.*

The Langhorne sisters were not the only famous people to be born in Danville. Among the others (certainly not all) are Wendell Scott, the first African American NASCAR driver; Camilla Williams, the first African American to sign a contact with New York City Opera; Eric Owens, former Major League baseball player; Tony Rice, bluegrass musician; and Charles Tyner, actor.[280]

During its heyday, when the mills and the factories were booming, Danville was a mecca, drawing people from the countryside and from nearby North Carolina. Residents of Caswell County, North Carolina, "sold their tobacco in Danville and shopped there for items not available in Yanceyville or Milton." They came to Danville on movie dates or when a hospital was needed. They, too, worked in the textile mills in Danville.[281]

In recent years, Danville has fallen on hard times with first the sale and then the demise of Dan River Mills. The once bustling downtown streets

Bridge at Riverwalk Trail, Danville. *Photo by Alice Green.*

Graves in Freedman's Cemetery, Danville. *Photo by Alice Green.*

Green Hill Cemetery, Danville. *Photo by Alice Green.*

are quiet and deserted at night. As in many cities, businesses have moved out from the city center. The anchor stores have moved out to the mall. Shopping centers are on Riverside Drive and Piney Forest Road. At the same time, the city has expanded past its bounds so that what was once "country" is now "suburbs."

Danville has had the highest rate of unemployment in the state. But the city shows signs of recovery. The Goodyear Tire and Rubber Company still has a plant located in Danville. City officials have actively sought to bring in new businesses (such as the Swedish company Ikea) and form new partnerships (such as the Institute for Advanced Learning and Research, operated by Virginia Tech in conjunction with academic partners Averett University and Danville Community College) for research, education and community outreach.

For local residents and visitors to the city, there is a waterfront park and museums (including the Danville Museum of Fine Arts and History, located in the former Sutherlin Mansion). Historic markers throughout the city recall the past, from the tobacco warehouse district and Confederate Prison No. 6 to the Holbrook-Ross neighborhood, where the black commercial-civic elite had their homes. There are also the graves in the Freedman's

Doyle J. Thomas Park, Danville. *Photo by Alice Green.*

Islamic Center of Danville, South Union Street. *Photo by Alice Green.*

Danville Police Department patrol car, 2010. *Photo by Alice Green.*

Cemetery, adjacent to the Green Hill Cemetery. The cemetery for free blacks and former slaves was established in 1872, but now only about thirty of the original markers remain.[282] But there is a marker located near the courthouse recalling "Bloody Monday," when police launched an assault against civil rights demonstrators.

On its website, the Danville Police Department offers these thoughts about that summer of 1963:

> *Charged with the responsibility of upholding and enforcing the law using techniques and tactics common at the time, the police performed these duties but not without controversy. The experience gained during this trying period of civil unrest began to shape the police department in many different ways, as evidenced by the writings of Detective Captain Jubal E. Towler, whose published works still offer sound advice in the use of practical police procedures.*[283]

As this historian of the Danville Police Department notes, the civil rights movement marked a turning point in the city's history. Today, Danville faces other challenges. But Danville has endured as a community and is a city poised to rebound in the twenty-first century.

Notes

Chapter 1

1. Hamm, *Murder, Honor, and Law*, 66–67, 71. The account of Moffett's shooting is taken from the chapter in this book titled "A Danville Difficulty." Hamm provided an earlier account of the case in his article "Killing of John Moffett and the Trial of J.T. Clark."
2. Hamm, "Danville Difficulty," 73.
3. Ibid., 74.
4. Ibid., 75–76.
5. Ibid., 77.
6. Ibid., 77–78.
7. Ibid., 79–88.
8. Ibid., 89.
9. Clement, *History of Pittsylvania County*.
10. Hagan, *Story of Danville*.
11. Fountain, *Danville, Virginia*.
12. Robertson, "Diary of a Southern Refugee," n. 126, 223.
13. Fountain, *Danville, Virginia*, 8.
14. Mainwaring, "Community in Danville, Virginia," 60.
15. See Bird (2003) for discussion.
16. Hagan, *Story of Danville*.
17. Robertson, "Danville under Military Occupation," 1967.
18. Ricketts, "Arsenal Explosion in Danville," 1865.
19. Pulley, *Old Virginia Restored*.
20. Ibid., 41.

21. Ibid., 41–43; Wynes, *Race Relations in Virginia*.

22. Bodine, "Readjuster Movement"; Higginbotham, "Danville Riot of Nov. 3, 1883"; Tate, "Danville Riot of 1883."

23. Mainwaring, "Community in Danville, Virginia," 66.

24. U.S. Congress, Senate, *Alleged Outrages*, ix (hereafter U.S. Senate Report).

25. U.S. Senate Report, vi–ix.

26. Tate, "Danville Riot of 1883," 56–57.

27. U.S. Senate Report.

28. *New York Times*, "The Danville Fracas," November 6, 1883, 6.

29. U.S. Senate Report.

30. Shapiro, *White Violence and Black Response*, 24–25.

31. King, *Robert Addison Schoolfield*, 31.

32. Ibid., 26.

33. Ibid., 25, 27.

34. Simpson, *Men, Places and Things in Danville*.

Chapter 2

35. Smith, *As a City Upon a Hill*.

36. Simpson, *Men, Places and Things in Danville*, 276.

37. *Danville Register*, "Danville Had Good Year," January 1, 1905, 1, 3.

38. Ibid., 3.

39. See Smith, "Mill on the Dan," for more on the biographies of the founders of the mills.

40. Hagan, *Story of Danville*, 5.

41. *Danville Register*, "Local Option Danville," March 1, 1905, 2.

42. Simpson, *Men, Places and Things in Danville*, 33.

43. *Danville Register*, May 1924.

44. See Mainwaring, "Community in Danville, Virginia."

45. *Danville Register*, February 1922.

46. *Danville Register*, quoted in Mainwaring, "Community in Danville, Virginia."

47. *Danville Register*, "Local Option Danville," March 1, 1905, 2.

48. *Danville Register*, "Negro Anti-Saloon League," February 28, 1909, 8.

49. *Danville Register*, May 3, 1911.

50. *Danville Register*, "Prohibition and the Negro Vote," December 24, 1910, 4.

51. Moger, *Virginia: Bourbonism to Byrd*, 312.

52. Hagan, *Story of Danville*.

53. Moger, *Virginia: Bourbonism to Byrd*, 302.

54. Ibid., 319.

55. Ibid., 298.

56. Ibid., 311–12.

57. Brownell, *Urban Ethos in the South*.

58. Ibid., 58.

59. Lebsock, *Murder in Virginia*, 110.

60. *Richmond Planet*, "A Silver Wedding," September 21, 1907.

61. *Richmond Planet*, May 17, 1913.

62. *Richmond Planet*, "Editor Mitchell in Danville," January 10, 1914.

63. *Richmond Planet*, July 4, 1908.

64. *Richmond Planet*, "Danville News," March 9, 1918.

65. *Richmond Planet*, "Danville News," April 13, 1918.

66. *Richmond Planet*, "Vital Question Asked By Attorney Carter," April 28, 1917.

67. *Richmond Planet*, "Notes by the Way," July 19, 1902.

68. *Danville Register*, December 26, 1909.

69. *Richmond Planet*, "Editor Mitchell's Travels," November 26, 1904.

70. *Richmond Planet*, March 11, 1911.

71. *Richmond Planet*, "Trouble in Danville, VA," October 20, 1917.

72. *Danville Register*, "Favorably Received Here," July 18, 1906.

73. *Richmond Planet*, July 7, 1900.

74. *Danville Register*, "A Time for Coolness and Self-Control," July 31, 1917, 4.

75. Danville City Council Minutes, April 13, 1915.

76. *Danville Register*, "To Show Famous Film," October 28, 1915, 6.

77. George, "Policing Miami's Black Community," 434–50.

78. Chalmers, *Hooded Americanism*, 230.

79. Ibid., 231.

80. *Danville Register*, March 26, 1922, 7.

81. *Danville Register*, July 15, 1924.

82. *Danville Register*, "K.K.K. Befriend Stranger Here," April 29, 1922, 5.

83. *Danville Register*, "Negro Who Pursued White Woman Shot Dead After Coming Back Second Time," March 1, 1921, 1.

84. *Danville Register*, "A Vigorous Policy Demanded," March 1, 1921, 4.

85. *Danville Register*, "Neither Occasion nor Demand for It," May 12, 1921, 6.

86. *Danville Register*, "For Better Racial Relations, May 13, 1921, 6.

87. *Danville Register*, May 1921.

88. Although the name is spelled differently, this is probably E.G. Moseley.

89. *Danville Register*, "Mosely's Klan Resolution Was Defeated," July 13, 1923, 3.

90. Moger, *Virginia: Bourbonism to Byrd*, 55.

CHAPTER 3

91. *Danville Register*, "Grand Jury Probe Fails to Show City Lawless," February 11, 1921, 1.

92. *Danville Register*, "Colored Ministers Deplore Crime Wave," March 17, 1921, 2.

93. Bailey, "Boundary Maintenance."

94. Danville Common Council Minutes, Charter and Ordinance, 1907.

95. Hagan, *Story of Danville*.

96. *Danville Register*, "Both Sides Preparing," January 1, 1905, 2.

97. *Danville Register*, "Criticised the Police," January 24, 1905, 2.

98. *Danville Register*, "Whiskey Cases Dismissed," January 4, 1905, 6.

99. Ibid.

100. *Danville Register*, "Alleged Liquor Venders," February 17, 1905, 2.

101. Ibid.

102. Ibid.

103. *Danville Register*, "More Blind Tigers Raided," February 19, 1905.

104. Danville City Council Minutes; *Danville Register*.

105. Danville City Council Minutes, 1905.

106. Ibid., October 1905.

107. Danville Corporation Court Records, February 1907.

108. *Danville Register*, "Chief Morris Fined $5," January 12, 1908, 2.

109. *Danville Register*, "Chief Morris Reprimanded," March 7, 1909, 2.

110. *Danville Register*, "Chief of Police Acquitted," February 25, 1909.

111. *Danville Register*, January 28, 1911.

112. Ibid.

113. *Danville Register*, "Police Chief Proves to Be Convict," March 3, 1911, 1.

114. Ibid.

115. *Danville Register*, "Lesson of the Local Sensation," March 4, 1911, 4.

116. *Danville Register*, April 1908.

117. *Danville Register*, March 1909.

118. *Danville Register*, "Hail to the New Chief," March 4, 1911, 4.

119. *Danville Register*, February 1922.

120. *Danville Register*, January 1922.

121. *Danville Register*, June 21, 1921.

122. *Danville Register*, May 2, 1924.

123. *Danville Register*, March 1925.

124. *Danville Register*, "Smallest Number of Drunks in Years," June 2, 1926, 3.

125. *Danville Register*, "Police Land Many Drunks on Wild Saturday Night," September 4, 1927, 2.

126. *Danville Register*, "More Blind Tigers Raided," February 10, 1909; see also "17 Blind Tigers Raided," February 9, 1909, 2.

127. *Danville Register*, February 10, 1909.

128. *Danville Register*, "'Jack' Robinson Guilty," January 28, 1905, 6 (note: appears as 1904).

129. Musto, *American Disease*, 6.

130. Ibid.

131. Ibid., 7.

132. Ibid.

133. Ibid., 8.

134. Ibid., 19.

135. *Danville Register*, "Sale of Cocaine," January 8, 1908, 5.

136. *Danville Register*, "Cocaine Sellers Liberated," March 16, 1910, 2.

137. Towler, *Evil We Seek*, 37.

138. *Danville Register*, "An Ordinance Prohibiting Gambling in the City of Danville," July 19, 1906.

139. *Danville Register*, October 17, 1906.

140. *Danville Register*, February 9, 1908.

141. *Danville Register*, "Women Are Summoned," October 24, 1913, 8.

142. *Danville Register*, "Commend the Mayor," March 4, 1915, 2.

143. *Danville Register*, "Women Say They Are Neglected," March 4, 1919, 1.

144. *Danville Register*, "A Local Problem Calmly Reviewed," March 5, 1919, 4.

145. Danville City Council Minutes, 1919.

146. Hagan, *Story of Danville*.

147. *Danville Register*, "Banish the Idle Negro," November 28, 1909, 4.

148. *Danville Register*, "Crusade Against Vagrants," April 20, 1909, 2.

149. *Danville Register*, "Vagrants Before Mayor," October 26, 1909, 6.

150. Danville City Council Minutes, December 1917.

151. Ibid., 1913.

152. *Danville Register*, July 28, 1914.

153. *Danville Register*, July-September, 1934.

154. These photos are not included here because of a problem with resolution. However, our thanks to the Danville Police Department for approving their use.

CHAPTER 4

155. Link, 237–42.

156. Ibid.

157. NAACP, *Thirty Years of Lynching*, 29.

158. Shay, *Judge Lynch*, 273–74.

159. Perrett, *America in the Twenties*, 245–56.

160. *Richmond Planet*, "Lynchers Foiled in Danville," July 30, 1904.

161. Ibid.

162. *Danville Register*, February 21, 1905.

163. *Richmond Planet*, August 6, 1904, editorial page.

164. Ibid.

165. *Richmond Planet*, "Trouble in Danville, VA," October 20, 1917.

166. *Danville Register*, "Mob Riddles Negro Who Slew Officer and Wounded Six Men," October 13, 1917, 1. The *Register* provided extensive and detailed coverage of the incident.

167. Ibid.

168. NAACP, 101.

169. *Danville Register*, "Not a Lynching in Any Sense," October 14, 1917, 4.

170. *Danville Register*, "Mob Riddles Negro Who Slew Officer and Wounded Six Men," October 13, 1917, 1.

171. *Danville Register*, July 19, 1906.

172. See *Danville Register*, "Negroes Go North," April 20, 1909, 2. The newspaper reported that "about five hundred" blacks from the Danville area left the day before on a special train headed for Newburgh, New York. The blacks had been recruited by an agent to work in brick factories. This had been the third group of blacks to leave in the past few days.

173. Bailey, "Boundary Maintenance."

174. *Danville Register*, December 1915.

175. *Richmond Planet*, "Danville Soldiers Prevented," July 30, 1917.

176. Ibid.

177. *Danville Register*, "Negro Citizens Speak Out," July 31, 1917, 2.

178. *Danville Register*, "A Time For Coolness And Self-Control," July 31, 1917, 4.

179. *Richmond Planet*, "Negro's Insult Resented," August 4, 1917.

180. Ibid.

181. *Danville Register*, June 1921; also see Tangen, "Spring Guns."

182. *Danville Register*, "Alleged Assault Case," February 9, 1905, 2.

183. *Danville Register*, "Will Protect The Banks," January 1, 1915.

184. *Danville Register*, "Held for Robbing Store," October 26, 1909.

185. *Danville Register*, January 12, 1905, 2.

186. *Danville Register*, "Fight on Main Street," October 26, 1909, 2.

187. *Danville Register*, "Clem Cousins Killed by His Father-in-Law, E.C. Smith, on Union Street in Drunken Row," 1.

188. See Kennedy, *Race, Crime, and the Law*.

CHAPTER 5

189. Mainwaring, "Community in Danville, Virginia."

190. Danville City Council Minutes; *Danville Register*, "The Jail Commissioners," January 6, 1905, 2.

191. Danville City Council Minutes.

192. *Danville Register*, August 1907.

193. Corporation Court Records.

194. Danville City Council Minutes, Charter and Ordinance, 1907.

195. *Danville Register*, "Jail Inspector's Report," January 12, 1908.

196. *Danville Register*, January 1908.

197. Danville City Council Minutes, 1908.

198. *Danville Register*, "Steel Cages Arrive," February 19, 1909, 2.

199. *Danville Register*, February 2, 1910.

200. Danville City Council Minutes, 1910.

201. Danville City Council Minutes, May 1911.

202. Ibid., June 1915.

203. *Danville Register*, November 1917.

204. *Danville Register*, 1921.

205. *Danville Register*, May 1922.

206. *Danville Register*, July 1922.

207. Danville City Council Minutes, March 4, 1925, and July 29, 1926.

208. *Danville Register*, 1934.

209. *Danville Register*, "Children of the Streets," January 13, 1905, 2.

210. *Danville Register*, 1918.

211. Danville City Council Minutes, May 9, 1922.

212. Ibid., November 7, 1922, and December 5, 1922.

213. Ibid., 1923.

214. Ibid., June 29, 1926.

CHAPTER 6

215. Dredge, "Contradictions of Corporate Benevolence," 308–326.

216. Ibid., 308.

217. Ibid.

218. *Danville Register*, "Association For Women," January 13, 1905, 3.

219. *Christian Science Monitor*, "Cotton Mills Give Employees a Voice," July 15, 1919, 5.

220. Heinemann, *Depression and New Deal*, 6.

221. Mainwaring, "Community in Danville, Virginia," 131–34.

222. Ibid., 153.

223. See Mainwaring, "Community in Danville, Virginia."

224. Heinemann, 8.

225. Ibid., 8–9.

226. Mainwaring, "Community in Danville, Virginia," 284.

227. Ibid., 284.

228. Ibid., 290.

229. *Encyclopedia Virginia*, "Dan River Mills."

230. Mainwaring, "Community in Danville, Virginia."

231. *New York Times*, "Rejects Strike Mediation," October 4, 1930, 17.

232. Martin-Perdue and Perdue, *Talk About Trouble*, 288.

233. Ibid., 288–89.

234. Mainwaring, "Community in Danville, Virginia."

235. Heinemann, 31.

236. *New York Times*, "Cotton Fabric Group to Seek Protection," January 18, 1935, 38.

237. Heinemann, 19.

238. Roberts, "New Cure for Brightleaf Tobacco," 32.

239. Ibid., 39–40.

240. Heinemann, 37.

241. *Danville Register*, July–September 1943.

242. See Mainwaring, "Community in Danville, Virginia."

243. *New York Times*, "C.I.O. Leaders Clash," September 13, 1950, 22.

244. *New York Times*, "Dan River Fears Losses," March 9, 1951, 44.

245. *New York Times*, "Union Scores Pay Rise [sic],"April 17, 1951, 23.

246. *New York Times*, "Struck Mills Reject Arbitration Offer," April 21, 1951, 20.

247. *New York Times*, "Gun Battle Marks Cotton Mills' Strike," April 28, 1951, 21.

248. Mainwaring, "Community in Danville, Virginia," 332.

249. Whitfield, "The 'Golden' Era of Civil Rights," 39; Cresswell," Last Days of Jim Crow in Southern Libraries," 559.

250. *Encyclopedia Virginia*, "Danville Civil Rights Demonstrations"; see also "A Guide to the 1963 Danville (VA) Civil Rights Cases. A Collection in the Library of Virginia." http://www.lva.virginia.gov/findaid/38099.htm.

251. *Encyclopedia Virginia*, "Danville Civil Rights Demonstrations of 1963."

252. Ibid.

253. *New York Times*, June 16, 1963, 58.

254. For discussion see Holt, *Act of Conscience*, 1965. Holt served as one of the defense attorneys. Other defense attorneys included Ruth Harvey, Jerry Williams and Henry L. Wood.

255. Miller and Lyon, SNCC pamphlet, August 1963. For discussion of SNCC use of photographs, see Raiford, "Come Let Us Build."

256. *New York Times*, June 13, 1963, 1.

257. *New York Times*, "35 Are Jailed in Danville, Va., As Negroes Defy Protest Ban," June 16, 1963, 58.

258. *New York Times*, "Danville Parleys Yield a New Calm," June 18, 1963, 34.

259. *New York Times*, "Danville Talk Unproductive," June 21, 1963, 12.

260. *New York Times*, "Danville's Police Seize 3 in Church," June 23, 1963, 62.

261. *New York Times*, "Dr. King Steps Up Danville Protest," July 12, 1963, 8.

262. *New York Times*, "100 Foes of Segregation Picket Virginia Concern's Local Office," July 18, 1963, 10.

263. *New York Times*, "Threat in Danville," July 31, 1963, 13.

264. *New York Times*, "U.S. Court Balks Danville Trials,"August 9, 1963, 9.

265. *New York Times*, "Danville Jury Resumes," August 15, 1963, 19.

266. *New York Times*, "Danville Drops a Racial Attack," September 24, 1963, 29.

267. *New York Times*, First Negro Hired By Danville Police," October 18, 1963.

268. *Encyclopedia Virginia*, "Danville Civil Rights Demonstrations of 1963"; see also "A Guide to the 1963 Danville (VA) Civil Rights Cases."

269. Minchin, "Black Activism," 809.

270. Ibid., 816.

271. Ibid., 818.

272. Ibid., 827.

273. Ibid., 837.

274. Fountain, *Danville, Virginia*, 8.

275. Ibid., 8.
276. *Danville Register*, May 23, 1988.

EPILOGUE

277. Cohen, "Robert W. Gordon," 20; see also *New York Times*, "A Train Falls 75 Feet," September 28, 1903.
278. For information about the show, see Tara Bozick, "History Channel Airs Hunt for Confederate Treasure in Danville," December 31, 2010. http://www2.wsls.com/news/2010/dec/31/history-channel-airs-hunt-confederate-treasure-dan-ar-746364.
279. *Encyclopedia Virginia*, "Irene Langhorne Gibson"; *New York Times*, "Lady Astor Dies; Sat in Commons," May 3, 1964, 1.
280. Wikipedia, "Danville, Virginia," http://en.wikipedia.org/wiki/Danville,_Virginia.
281. Caswell County Historical Association, private communication from Rick Frederick, archivist and webmaster.
282. Ricketts, "Arsenal Explosion in Danville, VA 1865."
283. Danville Police Department website, www.danville-va.gov/index.aspx?nid=588.

Bibliography

Bailey, Frankie Y. "Boundary Maintenance, Interest-Group Conflict, and Black Justice in Danville, Virginia, 1900–1930." Dissertation, School of Criminal Justice, State University of New York, Albany, New York, 1986.

Bird, Stephen V. "Heralding Economic and Political Independence: Danville, Virginia's Newspaper Editors Adopt James Gordon Bennett's Penny Press Model during the Civil War." *American Journalism* 20, no. 4 (2003): 55–82.

Bodine, Lee Howard. "The Readjuster Movement: Its Influence Upon Race Relations in Virginia." MA thesis, Smith College, 1965.

Brownell, Blaine A. *The Urban Ethos in the South, 1920–1930*. Baton Rouge: Louisiana State University Press, 1975.

Chalmers, David M. *Hooded Americanism: The First Century of The Ku Klux Klan, 1865–1965*. Garden City, NY: Doubleday & Co., 1965.

Clement, Maud Carter. *The History of Pittsylvania County, Virginia*. Lynchburg, VA: J. Bell Co., 1929.

Cohen, Norm. "Robert W. Gordon and the Second Wreck of 'Old 97.'" *Journal of American Folklore* 87, no. 343 (January–March 1974): 12–38.

Cresswell, Stephen. "The Last Days of Jim Crow in Southern Libraries." *Libraries & the Culture Record* 31 (1996): 557–73.

Dailey, Jane. *Before Jim Crow: The Politics of Race in Postemancipation Virginia*. Chapel Hill: University of North Carolina Press, 2000.

Davis, William C., and James I. Robertson Jr., eds. *Virginia at War, 1862*. Lexington: University Press of Kentucky, 2007.

Dredge, Bart. "Contradictions of Corporate Benevolence: Industrial Libraries in the Southern Textile Industry, 1920–1945." *Libraries & the Cultural Record* 43, no. 3 (2008): 308–26.

Encyclopedia Virginia. "Dan River Mills." Virginia Foundation for the Humanities. http://www.encyclopediavirginia.org/about.

———. "Danville Civil Rights Demonstrations of 1963." Virginia Foundation for the Humanities. http://www.encyclopediavirginia.org/about.

———. "Danville During the Civil War." Virginia Foundation for the Humanities. http://www.encyclopediavirginia.org/about.

———. "Irene Langhorne Gibson." Virginia Foundation for the Humanities. http://www.encyclopediavirginia.org/about.

———. "Richmond and Danville Railroad During the Civil War." Virginia Foundation for the Humanities. http://www.encyclopediavirginia.org/about.

Fountain, Clara. *Danville: A Pictorial History.* Virginia Beach, VA: Donning Co., 1979.

Fountain, Clara Garrett. *Danville, Virginia (Postcard History Series).* Charleston, SC: Arcadia Publishing, 2000.

George, Paul S. "Policing Miami's Black Community, 1896–1930." *Florida Historical Quarterly* 57, no. 4 (1979): 434–50.

Hagan, Jane Gray. *The Story of Danville.* New York: Stratford House, 1950.

Hamm, Richard F. *Murder, Honor, and Law: Four Virginia Homicides from Reconstruction to the Great Depression.* Charlottesville and London: University of Virginia Press, 2003.

———. "The Killing of John R. Moffett and the Trial of J.T. Clark: Race, Prohibition, and Politics in Danville, 1887–1893." *Virginia Magazine of History and Biography* 101, no. 3 (1993): 375–404.

Heinemann, Ronald L. *Depression and New Deal in Virginia: The Enduring Dominion.* Charlottesville: University Press of Virginia, 1983.

Higginbotham, Charmion Woody. "The Danville Riot of Nov. 3, 1883." MA thesis, Virginia State, 1955.

Holt, Len. *An Act of Conscience.* Boston: Beacon Press, 1965.

Kennedy, Randall. *Race, Crime, and the Law.* New York: Pantheon, 1997.

King, Robert. *Robert Addison Schoolfield (1853–1931).* Richmond, VA: William Byrd Press, 1979.

Lebsock, Suzanne. *A Murder in Virginia: Southern Justice on Trial.* New York: W.W. Norton, 2003.

Link, William A. *Roots of Secession: Slavery and Politics in Antebellum Virginia.* Chapel Hill and London: University of North Carolina Press, 2003.

Mainwaring, Thomas William, Jr. "Community in Danville, Virginia, 1880–1963." PhD dissertation, University of North Carolina at Chapel Hill, 1988.

Martin-Perdue, Nancy J., and Charles L. Perdue Jr., eds. *Talk About Trouble: A New Deal Portrait of Virginians in the Great Depression*. Chapel Hill: University of North Carolina Press, 1996.

Miller, Dorothy (text), and Danny Lyon (photographs). SNCC pamphlet, August 1963.

Minchin, Timothy J. "Black Activism, the 1964 Civil Rights Act, and the Racial Integration of the Southern Textile Industry." *Journal of Southern History* 63, no. 1 (1999): 809–844.

Moger, Allen W. *Virginia: Bourbonism to Byrd, 1870–1925*. Charlottesville: University Press of Virginia, 1968.

Moore, James T. "Black Militancy in Readjuster Virginia, 1879–1883. *Journal of Southern History* 41, no. 2 (1975): 167–86.

Musto, David F. *The American Disease: Origins of Narcotic Control*. New Haven and London: Yale University Press, 1973.

NAACP. *Thirty Years of Lynching in the United States: 1889–1918*. New York: Arno Press and the New York Times, 1969.

Perrett, Geoffrey. *America in the Twenties*. New York: Simon and Schuster, 1982.

Pulley, Raymond H. *Old Virginia Restored, 1870–1939*. Charlottesville: University of Virginia Press, 1968.

Raiford, Leigh. "'Come Let Us Build a New World Together': SNCC and Photography of the Civil Rights Movement." *American Quarterly* 59, no. 4 (2007): 1129–57.

Ricketts, Danny. "Arsenal Explosion in Danville, VA 1865." http://arsenalexplosion.blogspot.com.

Roberts, Blain. "A New Cure for Brightleaf Tobacco: The Origins of the Tobacco Queen during the Great Depression." *Southern Cultures* 12, no. 2 (2006): 30–52.

Robertson, James I., Jr., ed. "Diary of a Southern Refugee during the War, January–June 1982 (Judith Brockenbrough McGuire)," in Davis and Robertson's *Virginia at War, 1862*, 155–227.

Robertson, James I. "Danville under Military Occupation." *Virginia Magazine* 75, no. 3 (July 1967).

Shapiro, Herbert. *White Violence and Black Response: From Reconstruction to Montgomery*. Amherst: University of Massachusetts Press, 1988.

Shay, Frank. *Judge Lynch: His First Hundred Years*. Montclair, NJ: Patterson Smith, 1969.

Simpson, Benjamin [pseud.] *Men, Places and Things in Danville*. Ed. Duval Porter. 1st ed. Danville, VA: Dance Bros. Printer, 1891.

Smith, Page. *As a City Upon a Hill*. New York: Alfred A. Knopf, 1966.

Smith, Robert S. "Mill on the Dan: Riverside Cotton Mills, 1882–1901." *Journal of Southern History* 21, no. 1 (1955): 38–66.

Tangen, Ed. "Spring Guns." *American Journal of Police Science* 1, no. 3 (1930): 307–312.

Tate, William Carrington, Jr. "The Danville Riot of 1883: Its Effects on Politics in Virginia." MA thesis, University of Richmond, Richmond, Virginia, 1968.

Towler, Juby E. *The Evil We Seek: A Biography of Capt'n Joe Lewis of the Danville Police Department.* Danville, Virginia, 1952.

U.S. Congress. Senate. Committee on Privileges and Elections. *Alleged Outrages.* 48th Cong., 1st sess., Report No. 579, Library of Congress, 1884, ix.

Whitfield, Stephen J. "The 'Golden' Era of Civil Rights Consequences of the Carolina Israelite." *Southern Culture* 14, no. 3 (2008): 26–51.

Wynes, Charles. *Race Relations in Virginia, 1870–1902.* Charlottesville: University of Virginia Press, 1961.

About the Authors

Frankie Y. Bailey is a native of Danville, Virginia. After graduating from Tunstall High School, she attended Virginia Tech, majoring in psychology and English. She received her MA and PhD from the School of Criminal Justice, University at Albany (SUNY). She is now a faculty member at the school, specializing in crime history, crime and mass media/popular culture. Her most recent nonfiction books are *African American Mystery Writers* (2008) and (with Alice P. Green) *Wicked Albany: Lawlessness & Liquor in the Prohibition Era* (2009). Bailey is the author of a mystery series featuring Virginia-based crime historian Lizzie Stuart.

Alice P. Green grew up a member of one of the few African American families in the small Adirondack mining town of Witherbee, New York. She has an MA in social work (University at Albany, SUNY, 1973) and an MA and PhD from the School of Criminal Justice (University at Albany, 1983). After holding several administrative positions with agencies, Green founded and serves as executive director of the Center for Law and Justice, a nonprofit community organization. In addition to being an adjunct professor, Green has been a candidate for political office and is a frequent writer/commentator on criminal justice issues.

Visit us at
www.historypress.net